The Power of Now

Real-Time Analytics and
IBM InfoSphere Streams

Jacques Roy

New York   Chicago   San Francisco
Athens   London   Madrid   Mexico City
Milan   New Delhi   Singapore   Sydney   Toronto

The Power of Now: Real-Time Analytics and IBM InfoSphere Streams

1 2 3 4 5 6 7 8 9 0   DOC DOC   1 0 9 8 7 6 5 4

ISBN   978-0-07-184337-9
MHID   0-07-184337-X

Sponsoring Editor
Paul Carlstroem

Editorial Supervisor
Patty Mon

Project Manager
Shruti Awasthi,
Cenveo® Publisher Services

Acquisitions Coordinator
Amanda Russell

Technical Editor
Robert Uleman

Copy Editor
Bart Reed

Proofreader
Lisa McCoy

Production Supervisor
Jean Bodeaux

Composition
Cenveo Publisher Services

Illustration
Cenveo Publisher Services

Art Director, Cover
Jeff Weeks

To the people who matter the most when it comes to IBM InfoSphere Streams: the InfoSphere Streams customers, present and future, the consultants helping them, and the InfoSphere Streams development team.

—Jacques Roy

About the Author

Jacques Roy is a member of the IBM Worldwide technical sales and enablement team, focusing on InfoSphere Streams. Over his decades in the industry, Jacques has worked in various roles, including consulting, development/development manager, and presales. He has also worked in many technology areas, including operating systems, databases, application servers, and application development with programming languages such as APL, C/C++, Java, PHP, JavaScript, and many more. He is the author of several books, redbooks, DeveloperWorks articles, and IBMdatamag.com articles. Jacques has also been a presenter at many conferences, including IBM's Information on Demand (IOD), now IBM Insight.

About the Technical Editor

Robert Uleman has been with IBM since 2001. Robert has been training IBMers and partners on InfoSphere Streams as well as working on Streams-based customer engagements since 2010. Previously, he focused on geospatial databases (Informix and DB2), with customers and in-product development. He has deep expertise in spatiotemporal computing and GIS, time series analysis, and image processing. Robert holds master's degrees in exploration geophysics (Stanford University) and applied physics (Delft University of Technology). He is based in California.

CONTENTS

ACKNOWLEDGMENTS

I'd first like to thank Paul Zikopoulos for giving me the opportunity to work on InfoSphere Streams in my second stint in the worldwide technical sales organization. The effort he put in to make it happen is much appreciated.

To Kimberly Madia, thank you for your perpetually positive attitude. I appreciate how quickly and enthusiastically you embraced this project and made it a reality. Thank you also for your comments on part of my draft content.

Thanks also go to Robert Uleman. I've known Robert for over 15 years now. How time flies. Robert was much more than a technical reviewer. He provided clarity, raised many questions, and contributed suggestions that have a major impact on how efficiently this book can convey its message. I am always amazed at his precise choice of words that help make the content so clear. I can't help but think about the title of a David Sedaris essay: "Me Talk Pretty One Day." In this book, I achieved a bit of this thanks to Robert.

Finally, thank you to the people who worked behind the scene to make this book a reality. This includes Susan Visser from IBM and the McGraw-Hill Education team, including Paul Carlstroem and Amanda Russell.

INTRODUCTION

Every so often, new technologies come out to answer changing business needs. We have seen this with relational databases, object-oriented programming, and web applications, just to name a few. IBM InfoSphere Streams falls into this category. It provides a new approach to processing information by providing an easy-to-program platform for distributed real-time analytics that can answer the need to generate information from the huge amount of data that comes at businesses rapidly.

This real-time approach requires a different way of thinking from the store-and-process (data-at-rest) method that is generally used. We need to change the way we think about data to see the opportunities offered by real-time processing. In some cases, the old approach can still do the job—but at what cost? We need to recognize that there are better ways to solve our business problems, and the real-time distributed analytics platform offered by InfoSphere Streams is a great tool to have in addition to using repositories with the store-and-process approach.

This book aims at answering questions such as the following:

- How does real-time distributed analytics fit into the big data challenge?

- How can I recognize opportunities to take advantage of this approach?

- What are the characteristics that make a good real-time distributed analytics platform?

- What does InfoSphere Streams offer?

- How do I get started?

This book is for people who want to understand distributed real-time analytics enough to recognize the opportunities in their enterprise to become more efficient at what they do and gain a business advantage. This can range from better production processes to better customer services.

This book is divided into six chapters that follow a logical progression.

Chapter 1 looks at the progression that led to the big data challenges, the differences between data at rest and data in motion, and the integration of multiple technologies to form a big data architecture that can process data, both at rest and in motion.

Chapter 2 presents use cases of distributed real-time analytics. It is interesting in and of itself, but the underlying goal is to present enough examples so you can start to see how this approach could apply to your environment. It covers general cases as well as several examples in different industries.

We can perform real-time analytics in multiple ways. The approach taken depends on how much data needs to be processed, the complexity of the processing, and how quickly we need to get to an answer. Chapter 3 looks at what it takes to develop a real-time distributed analytics solution and why we need to start with a proper platform with appropriate features.

Chapter 4 introduces InfoSphere Streams. This chapter stays at the functionality level to help architects, managers, and decision makers understand what the platform can do, what it includes out of the box, and how flexible it is in helping get to a business solution. This way, you can have a better idea of what can be done and the effort required to achieve it.

A distributed real-time analytics platform cannot live in a vacuum, and InfoSphere Streams is no exception. You need to understand how Streams fits within the existing enterprise architecture. This is the role of Chapter 5. This chapter describes the many ways InfoSphere Streams can interact with all sorts of systems—from file systems to network connections. It is not just an issue of connectivity, but also of speaking the same language. Streams can manipulate XML and JSON as well as talk to different messaging servers. It also interfaces with specialized libraries to process varied data without having to start from scratch. Knowing these possibilities makes it easier to imagine a solution.

Finally, Chapter 6 assumes you are interested in getting your feet wet and trying InfoSphere Streams. This chapter provides information on where to get Streams, the approach to take in learning it, and how to navigate multiple sources of information to get up to speed as fast as possible.

The book ends with an appendix that provides resources and references to help you get the information you need to become fluent with InfoSphere Streams.

Technology changes rapidly, and there is so much of it to learn. Hopefully, this book gives you a shortcut to becoming proficient with InfoSphere Streams so that you can dive into implementing a solution for your enterprise.

1

Big Data:
At Rest and in Motion

Data in motion does not live in a vacuum. It is part of an overall solution for the big data challenge. Before we can dive into this subject, we need to put it into context with a general discussion on big data.

This chapter takes a look at the origins of big data and talks about the different technologies used to solve the big data challenge. Because a big data solution must consider existing business solutions, we also look at the role of relational databases in this environment. We continue by looking at what is needed in a big data architecture, followed by the need for data-in-motion processing.

Where Does Big Data Come From?

We could say that big data has been around for a long time. In information management there were always challenges due to the amount of data people wanted to analyze and what the technology could support at the time. The amount of data kept increasing with hardware capacity. Computer memory went from kilobytes to megabytes—and now terabytes. The same happened with disk technology. CPU power doubled roughly every 18 months, and memory and disk capacity doubled every two years. So, what changed with the advent of big data?

You could arguably trace the origin of big data to the rise of the Internet and web browsers, but one useful definition came out in 2008 with the

1

introduction of the concept of a smarter planet: Instrumented, Interconnected, Intelligent.

In addition to the Internet, sensors have become ubiquitous. With the technology advances, it is becoming easier and easier to use sensors everywhere. For example, four billion passive radio frequency identifiers (RFIDs) were sold in 2012 and six billion in 2013.[1] Now let's consider smartphones. A total of almost one billion phones were sold in 2013.[2] A smartphone includes all sorts of sensors and happens to be easily locatable and identifiable. All sort of information can be inferred by looking at the location of a smartphone, which other smartphones are around, and how long the phone stays in one location. All these phones are constantly connected. We can see some potential for a crowdsourcing type of information that takes advantage of the multiple smartphones transmitting their locations. This can help in areas such as city planning and traffic reporting and forecasting.

On the industrial side of things, we have all sorts of sensors for acoustic signals, vibration, humidity, temperature, acceleration, and so on. We find sensors in all sorts of machines, including hundreds of sensors in cars. Now that cars are becoming connected, all this information becomes available for many purposes. Sensors are found everywhere, including on railroad tracks and pipelines. More and more of the sensors are connected to a network. This follows the original vision: Instrumented and Interconnected. The result of the constant analysis of all this data is a new type of intelligence that can optimize their use, such as in energy smart grids, and improve our lives.

There is also an inordinate amount of data generated daily in the form of tweets, blogs, Facebook statuses, pictures, YouTube videos, and so on. All that data begs to be mined for information.

Every company, in all industries, wants to take advantage of this availability of data to generate usable information that will make them more efficient and give them a business advantage. New technologies have appeared to help exploit big data.

New Technologies

Over the last several years, we've seen many new technologies appear to answer the big data challenge, the most famous one being Hadoop.

The enabling technology for Hadoop was the availability of cheap commodity hardware that allowed for the use of a cluster of machines to perform parallel processing. Hadoop consists, at its core, of a distributed file system and a processing engine called map/reduce. This engine schedules map/reduce jobs that process large files divided into blocks. This potentially allows for massively parallel processing.

The files in a Hadoop cluster are divided into blocks that are replicated to multiple machines. This serves two purposes: reliability and scalability. If a disk drive fails, the duplicated blocks are there to ensure the data is not lost. With the availability of the same file block on multiple nodes in the cluster, one of the copies can be selected to put the processing closer to the data, and different blocks of the same file can be processed by different nodes in the cluster concurrently.

The basic Hadoop environment created the need for additional technologies, including the following:

- Resource managers (YARN)
- Synchronization and configuration services (Zookeeper)
- Schedulers
- Cluster computing framework (Spark)
- Data serialization (Avro)
- Workflow coordination (Oozie)
- File loader (Flume)
- Database loader (Sqoop)
- Languages to make it easier to write map/reduce programs (Pig and Jaql)
- Database or table abstractions (HCatalog, HBase, and Hive)

We can also see that new types of repositories can integrate into the Hadoop cluster environment. These new products usually fall into the category of NoSQL databases, some of the most notable being the following:

- Accumulo
- Cassandra
- CouchDB
- MongoDB

All of these NoSQL databases come with their own application programming interfaces (APIs) or languages, and some of these languages are SQL like. In fact, SQL is becoming popular for Hadoop processing as an easier method to analyze data than the creation of map/reduce jobs. Using an SQL engine also opens the door for additional optimization. A map/reduce job is a two-step process that takes input from files and writes results to files. A business analytical process usually includes many more steps. Saving the intermediary steps means writing them to files, which can greatly decrease the overall performance due to the extra I/O to disk. An SQL engine could use many mechanisms to avoid these writes because it considers the entire process and not only one step of the process at a time. Other technologies are appearing in the Hadoop environment to fill this need also.

With the rise of SQL as part of Hadoop processing, this raises the question: What about relational databases?

What About Relational Databases?

It seems that people have been wanting to kill relational database management systems (RDBMSs) as soon as they first appeared. At first, the argument was that they could not handle the amount of data used in enterprises due to the computer resources required to run these database systems. Some people even claimed that RDBMSs would require specialized hardware if they ever hoped to stand a chance in the enterprise. A company called Britton Lee created such hardware at the time.

Computers improved, new algorithms were implemented in RDBMSs, and eventually relational databases became the dominant repository for the enterprise. The two main attractions were a declarative language (SQL) instead of procedural and the flexibility of access to the information (the table model allowed access any which way, as opposed to the hierarchical and network models that assumed a specific access path).

A second wave of attacks came in the 1980s with the rise of object-oriented programming and the creation of object databases. Once again, relational databases were supposed to be inadequate and destined for the dustbin. They were no good at handling persisting object hierarchies, and the impedance mismatch between an object representation and how it would look in a relational database was just too much trouble for developers.

Programmers apparently did not want to be forced to define schemas and develop additional code to write the objects' state to relational tables. Still, the hype subsided and RDBMSs continued to dominate. They also became more flexible with extensibility features such as user-defined types (UDTs), user-defined functions (UDFs), and user-defined aggregates (UDAs). Even hardware-assisted RDBMSs have appeared to speed up data warehouses— the most prominent one being the IBM PureData System for Analytics (Netezza).

The offensive was revived in the mid-2000s with the creation of XML databases. XML was the new method for data exchange. This provided more flexibility and made it easier for companies to exchange information and evolve their model. The industry quickly made the jump from data exchange format to data repository. Using an XML repository made it simpler because a new version of an XML document with new elements and attributes could still be saved in the repository without worrying about those changes. This was referred to as "schema evolution." Once again, trade magazines were trumpeting the death of relational databases. IBM even added XML support into DB2 (pureXML) to answer the needs of these new types of applications. Eventually, XML schemas became the norm to enforce the XML definitions in their repositories. Many people decided to simply stick with relational schemas instead, and RDBMSs continued to dominate the market.

The latest assault on RDBMSs comes from the NoSQL movement. Many people look at this term and jump to the conclusion that we have to get rid of relational databases. The term does not mean "no SQL" but instead "not only SQL," so it is a complementary technology not aimed at replacing relational databases but at filling the gap where other approaches may be better. Of course, some vendors in the NoSQL market want to replace relational databases because they don't have an RDBMS as part of their portfolio. NoSQL databases come in many flavors with a mix of key-value, tabular, column-family, columnar, and JSON capabilities. They answer different needs, not just in data access, but in other areas as well, such as consistency requirements.

During all this time, RDBMSs have continually evolved. We now see systems with clustering capabilities, specialized hardware (for example, field-programmable gate arrays), and columnar and in-memory capabilities. Add to that the fact that most companies have decades of investments in applications and corporate data invested in RDBMSs,[3] and it is obvious they are not disappearing any time soon. In fact, if history is our guide, they will continue to thrive in helping answer the new challenges raised by the big data explosion. Relational database systems have to be an integral part of a big data architecture.

Big Data Architecture

A big data architecture has to take into account that an enterprise has multiple needs, including transaction processing systems, data warehouses/datamarts, and operational data stores, all for accounting, payroll, customer services, and so on.

These systems have been in use for years and have proven their value. In most cases there is no reason to replace them because they do what is needed and are stable. In many cases they must interact among each other and with a big data solution. Data can flow in both directions: data from the operational system may flow into the big data repository, and data collected from different sources may flow back into the warehouse systems, as well as possibly additional customer information to operational stores. A Hadoop-based big data solution must be able to accommodate these data-flow requirements.

Also, other issues must be addressed for the continuing well-being of the enterprise, such as information governance and security. Information governance includes defining the varied data sources and establishing their level of quality, creating one version of the truth, controlling data lifecycle, and so on. Security would include compliance, audit, access control, and more.

A big data architecture has to consider its data sources and their processing attributes. What this means is that you have to understand the format, quality, and processing requirements of each data source. For example, you would likely want to scrub the data to ensure its quality before putting it into your data warehouse. The quality of data is essential to the proper use of a data warehouse; otherwise, it is "garbage in, garbage out." For this reason, you may need multiple types of repositories, depending on the needs. This is illustrated in Figure 1-1. Some repositories would be used for exploration, others for transactions, and yet others to generate analytical models to help predict things such as your next best action. Finally, you also need to

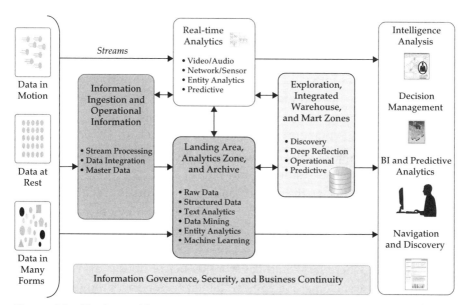

Figure 1-1 *Big data architecture*

understand how you will present the information you extract from your data, to whom, and how.

It makes sense to have an architecture that accounts for all the utilization possibilities, including how you get the information generated to the appropriate decision makers and in a format that is easily understood. Also, under all this, you need to consider the access and lifecycle of the data.

You don't have to implement the entire architecture all at once. In fact, in some cases, you may never implement it at all. The important point is that all potential processing requirements are covered by the architecture; therefore, if you need to add a new piece, you can have the peace of mind that everything will work together to achieve your business goals when you are ready to use these capabilities.

If you've noticed, the discussion up to this point has been about taking data and putting it in a repository before extracting information. This approach assumes you have the capacity to absorb the data coming at you as well as the capacity to store it all. It also means you are fine with extracting information from a snapshot of the state of your business. You need to figure out the potential cost of the latency between getting the data and generating actionable information.

The approach described up to this point (data at rest) is well known and has been used for decades. Relational databases have had the lion's share of the business data processing. The requirements for faster processing have pushed innovations into these products, going from clustering to hardware-assisted processing and in-memory capabilities. We've seen improvements in processing speeds that reduce the overall latency, but there is always more data to process that puts pressure on the current systems. What's more, there is still the issue of being able to store all the data coming at us, let alone whether it makes sense to store the raw data at all.

For example, look at the energy and utility industry. A lot of energy companies are implementing smart meters. These devices measure the amount of energy a customer consumes for a given period of time. Traditionally, meters were read once a month. A company employee would have his route where he would cover a number of houses every day. The reading of all the customer meters would then be done over roughly 20 days in a month. This means that if a company had 10 million customers, it would get around 500,000 readings every day of the week.

Now, with smart meters, energy companies are going from reading meters once a month to reading them once every 15 minutes. Some are even planning to read them more frequently. Reading the meters every 15 minutes means that a company will now collect in three hours what it used to collect in one year. Going back to our example, this means that its daily data collection goes from 500,000 readings to 960,000,000 readings. Once the company is able to get all the data in real time, it will get a burst of 10 million readings every 15 minutes. If it wants to do any type of analytics, this means the company will need to store the 10 million readings and then issue queries to that process, let's say, the last four hours of data (about 160 million readings) to get an accurate projection of the consumption on the energy grid, and then it will have to repeat this process at the next burst of readings.

It seems like such a waste of effort to write and then reread the data continuously. This is an example of where we are starting to see the need for processing data in motion. Coming back to our big data architecture, we can see that data-in-motion processing also plays a part, as shown in Figure 1-1. The data can flow directly to a landing zone or it can go through an in-motion processing engine, where the data is sent to the landing zone for storage and at the same time is analyzed in real time. The real-time analytics engine can then provide the result of the analysis to any other component of the architecture, including a user dashboard.

Data in Motion

Processing data in motion is different from processing data at rest. With data at rest, you always deal with a finite set of data. Not so with data in motion. In this model, we see a stream of data that has no beginning and no end. You have to decide if you want to process the pieces of data you are getting independently or in groups defined by time, range, or number.

To help in the discussion that follows, let's introduce the concept of an *operator*, which is an entity that represents processing. It may take zero or more inputs, and it operates on the input to generate processed output.

Let's get back to the meter-reading example from earlier. Each time we get a meter reading, we route it to an operator that takes care of writing it to the repository of our choice, but at the same time we route it to another set of operators that perform the analytics. Because the data is sent for real-time analytics, it is not necessary to keep the repository data up-to-date with the last reading immediately. We can optimize the process of writing the data to the repository by buffering it and wait until we have a more optimal amount of data before we write it. The reduction of I/O operations can have a huge impact on the ingestion capacity of a repository. The buffering in the real-time engine could accommodate a large amount of data by partitioning it over multiple nodes in a cluster.

This windowing capability is very powerful for continuing analysis. Let's say we want to use a four-hour window. The real-time processing engine collects the readings in a buffer, or window, that keeps track of the last 16 readings for each meter. When a new reading comes in, the oldest reading is discarded and the analytics is done based on the 16 readings in the window. One immediate application is that trends can be detected quickly and actions taken before a potential problem becomes a crisis. The analysis can be as simple as providing an instant value of the consumption at that interval or can be as complex as using linear regression algorithms or analytical models developed using historical data with tools such as SPSS.

Eliminating Noise and Reducing Volume

Earlier, I mentioned that the raw data may not need to be stored. Here is an example: you may be collecting status information from multiple pieces of equipment. A status may be provided at very short intervals (let's say 10 microseconds). You need to do the real-time analysis, but this does not mean you have to write it all to a repository. The status may not change at each interval. Therefore, only the changed values could be stored in the repository, or the values may be too fine-grained for the requirements. For historical purpose, values could be aggregated to, let's say, one-tenth of a second and stored as a record containing a count, high value, low value, and average. This way, the storage requirements drop by a factor of 10,000, thus greatly reducing the overall cost. This also means that the historical analysis would process much less data and therefore provide quicker results.

In other cases, you can filter the data based on specific criteria and discard what is not within those specifications. The result is less processing downstream and less storage required if the data is to be stored.

Real-Time Processing

I have mentioned real-time processing multiple times. Some could argue that real-time processing requires a specialized operating system that guarantees response time. This would be a strict interpretation of what "real time" is. A software application controlling a plane has strict requirements in response time, but in the big data world, real time is not as precise. For some, getting information within an hour instead of a day is real time.

In our context, it is probably better to talk about latency: how much time are you willing to wait between getting the data and taking action? The answer to this question varies depending on what you are trying to do. What we can see, though, is that the acceptable latency in a specific situation is getting smaller and smaller as time goes by. Companies that did not see a need for real-time processing a few years ago are starting to look at it. The next chapter provides some examples of places where data-in-motion processing can be applied.

Summary

In this chapter you learned that the volume of data has always caused problems, but today the mix of connected sensors, smartphones, and Internet social activities has caused an explosion of data that can be mined to generate insights, thus leading to new opportunities.

New technologies have appeared to answer the needs of big data analytics. However, they cannot be seen as wholesale replacements for existing systems or technologies. In many cases, they simply augment established systems that will continue to grow. It is important to look at a big data solution as including all the thriving legacy systems as well as the business requirements of governance and security.

Corporations continue to be under pressure to react more quickly to changing customer needs. There is more and more data to process and less time to convert it into actionable information. Processing data in motion can be a way to speed up this process and gain a competitive advantage.

Data-in-motion processing is more than a strategic business advantage. More and more, it is becoming a business necessity due to the rate of data ingestion and how quickly data can become stale and lose its usefulness. Data-in-motion processing will become an imperative for most corporations in the future.

Endnotes

1. http://www.rfid24-7.com/2014/03/13/rfid-market-exceeds-9b-in-2014-retail-drives-strong-growth/

2. http://www.gartner.com/newsroom/id/2665715

3. http://www.infoworld.com/t/dbms/not-so-fast-nosql-sql-still-reigns-244507

2

Big Data: In-Motion Use Cases

All data processing starts with data in motion, which can be as simple as taking the data and putting it in a repository. This chapter explores data in motion to help you better understand how it can be used to provide insights that can create a business advantage as well as new opportunities.

Here's what we'll discuss in this chapter:

- **Processing principles** The processing principles establish some high-level guidelines that can help us figure out which problems could be good candidates for data-in-motion processing.

- **Big data use cases** The big data use cases look at cross-industry-type problems and focus specifically on the ones that relate to our main subject.

- **Internet of Things** No discussion would be complete without talking about the Internet of Things (IoT). This section explores what it is and why it is so important to all businesses.

- **Use cases by industry** Finally, this chapter provides data-in-motion use cases for specific industries.

Processing Principles

The previous chapter provided one example of data in motion. How do we decide which problem is a good candidate for data-in-motion processing? If we look at the overall processing requirements, we could boil it down to two simple questions:

- Does using data in motion reduce our processing costs?
- Does using data in motion solve the problem of getting information from our data faster?

The second question also extends to the increasing volume of data that companies have to process. As the data increases, it puts more pressure on how quickly information can be derived from it. In some cases, especially at the beginning, the question can be answered by throwing more hardware at the problem—which then brings us back to question number one.

In programming, the fastest code is the one that is not there. It is also the easiest to maintain. We can apply this tongue-in-cheek statement to data. The fastest data processing is processing data that is not there. This may sound funny, but this concept is at the core of most systems. Look at relational database systems. The use of indexes allows the system to eliminate a large amount of data before the real processing is done. The result is getting to the answer faster.

In our case, we want to ask ourselves, what do we need to do with that data? An extreme answer would be, "nothing." At that point, we simply get rid of it. The real answer varies based on the data being discussed. The rest of this section looks at multiple conditions where data-in-motion processing can help.

Data Exhaust

Dictionary.com provides the following definition for data exhaust:

> "Unstructured information or data that is a by-product of the online activities of Internet users: Collecting and analyzing data exhaust can provide valuable insight into the purchasing habits of consumers."

This definition is a bit narrow. It can be expanded to all online activities, including social media activities. If we add to that all the machine-generated data, such as logs, we can see that a lot of data can be mined to find new opportunities for products and services, new process optimizations, and faster root-cause analysis leading to problem resolution.

The volume of data can raise questions such as the following:

- How much storage is needed to store all that data?

- How quickly can we process the data to generate actionable information?

- How much of this data is actually useful?

This last question is a great starting point. We are looking at unstructured data coming from varied sources. As we receive it, we can process it and decide what to keep and what to throw away. Even if we do not throw the data away, there are many cases where it can be analyzed on the fly to generate structured data that could be much smaller than the unstructured original. Finally, the upfront analysis can generate insights leading to changes in the business processing.

Doing the processing and analysis up front can have a large impact on storage requirements and therefore costs. Having less data stored also means faster processing, thus leading to faster insights, possibly through smaller overall machine resources.

Data exhaust is a good candidate for data-in-motion processing to generate quicker actionable information and reduce the overall cost of big data analytics.

Aggregation

There are situations where the data packets arrive with great frequency (in some cases, even microseconds). There is a need to analyze this data, but not necessarily to store it in its original format.

The following example is not an aggregation per se, but it allows us to greatly reduce the amount of data stored in a repository. Let's say we have a piece of equipment that produces statuses at very short intervals. For historical analysis purposes, we want to store these statuses in a repository. If the status is reported on a regular interval but does not change often, it would make sense to compare the new status to the previous one, and if they are the same, we simply discard the new. This way, what is then stored in the database would be the changes in the status. We can easily imagine the impact: if the status changes only every 100 readings, we are storing 100 times less data in the database.

A slight variation on the previous example is to allow a small percentage of variation. If the new value is within the accepted range, we could consider it the same as the previous value and discard it instead of storing it in the database.

There are cases where the data comes in so quickly that it is impractical to store it "as is" for historical analysis. The analysis has to be done in real time, but it may still be useful to keep an aggregation of the data for historical analysis. For example, the machine data may be arriving at microsecond-level intervals. Therefore, instead of storing it, we could aggregate it to a one-tenth-of-a-second interval. The values stored could then be the minimum, maximum, average, and count for all the values received during that time period. This provides a way for us to still perform historical analysis and, in this case, store roughly 10,000 times less data.

Because of the real-time capabilities of a data-in-motion solution, we can find a balance in the amount of historical data that needs to be kept and analyzed without compromising on the detailed analytics.

Transformation

The aggregation discussed in the previous section is a form of transformation. Many types of transformation can be done on data. Unstructured data can be analyzed as it is received and transformed into structured information—for example, by extracting specific words or group of words in context to generate buzz or sentiment information. The end result can then be stored in a repository as structured information for more efficient historical analysis. The extraction of buzz and sentiment could also reduce the overall size of the data, providing similar savings as the aggregation discussed earlier. Space saving is not the primary goal. In some cases, the original data and the transformed data could be saved in different repositories, serving different purposes.

Semi-structured data such as data in JavaScript Object Notation (JSON) format can also be processed to extract the elements our solution cares about and eliminate the extra data. This reduces the overall processing and storage load for the rest of the solution, resulting again in faster processing and decreased storage requirements. Note that the reduction in storage has other side effects, such as reducing the load on the different aspects of data governance.

Another type of transformation is enrichment. The incoming data may not be complete enough to make decisions on it. Additional information may be required. For example, this could be additional customer information coming from a database based on a customer identifier in the data.

Correlation

Many different inputs may need to be analyzed together to get to a decision on what needs to be done next. One stream of values by itself may indicate some possible actions but can be incomplete and lead to premature reactions. A specific machine signal in isolation may be monitored in too narrow a range in isolation to be effective, but with comparisons to the monitoring of other signals and indicators, it could provide a more effective alarm system for actionable information.

The type of data monitored and correlated can be varied. For example, in trading systems, a company stock price variation can be correlated with weather information and with news feeds to lead to a more efficient decision on what to do with a current stock position.

Continuous Analysis

Correlating data from multiple data sources, as just described, is an example of continuous analysis. Many situations lend themselves to continuous analysis. For example, if we are doing buzz and sentiment analysis, there are significant downsides to storing the data first in a repository and then launching the analysis. If we do that, we have to either figure out how to coordinate the writing of the data to disk with starting the analysis or use a time interval to relaunch the analysis on a regular schedule.

Landing the data in a repository means that new data is now part of a bigger pool. When re-reading the data, we need to either read a lot more data than required or use an indexing method to pinpoint the exact records we want to process. Using an index also adds processing because the range of values (likely based on a timestamp in our example) adds processing in terms of disk I/O to retrieve index pages and in computing cycles to perform the index value comparisons to identify the candidate records. Once this is done, our system then reads the data we want to analyze.

Many repositories such as database systems will cache some of the information to reduce I/O. Still, all that extra processing means we require larger systems than if we could simply keep track of a window of values in real time. Because we have to launch this processing at relatively short intervals, it multiplies the overhead required to get to our answer.

In the case of machine data analysis, the analysis may have to be done at intervals measured in seconds if not fractions of a second. Storing the data first before doing the analysis would not only cause a high overhead but, in some cases would make the analysis impossible to do.

Performing continuous analysis in a data-in-motion system does not mean that we do not store this data. It is a complementary approach to address specific requirements. Other requirements may need the data in a repository. That data could be stored "as is" or may benefit from other preprocessing, such as filtering, aggregation, and transformation.

Big Data Use Cases

IBM has identified five key use cases for big data analytics:

- Big data exploration
- Enhanced 360° view of the customer
- Security/intelligence extensions
- Operations analysis
- Data warehouse modernization

This section looks at these topics and how they could benefit from data-in-motion processing. The integration of data in motion in the big data use cases is another example of why real-time analytics should be part of a big data architecture.

Big Data Exploration

The goal of big data exploration is to experiment and see if we can extract new and valuable information from our data. Data scientists come up with business questions and try to answer them based on the historical data available to them. Answering these questions can uncover new relationships between different types of data and provide new insights on business opportunities.

Big data exploration often needs a flexible repository to host the data and make the querying easier. The IBM InfoSphere BigInsights solution is such a repository. It is a Hadoop-based solution that provides multiple interfaces to interrogate the data, such as a rich SQL interface and text analytics capabilities.

The exploration often requires access to all sorts of repositories, including an InfoSphere BigInsights landing zone, data warehouses and datamarts, and so on. Limiting the exploration to a Hadoop-type repository would reduce the visibility of the global enterprise. In this case, a solution such as IBM Watson Explorer is an ideal tool to group all the repositories into one global exploration pool. Watson Explorer also shares the same text analytics capability available in BigInsights and can process structured, semi-structured, and unstructured data.

Obviously, big data exploration is a data-at-rest problem. A data-in-motion solution can play a role in this context by providing the capabilities of processing the real-time data sources that feed these repositories. The role is complementary because it can generate actionable information from the data feeds. At the same time, it can filter, aggregate, transform, and correlate the data to put it in a more manageable form for the landing zone.

Enhanced 360° View of the Customer

The need to understand customers better keeps increasing with the availability of new technologies and new customer behavior. We have to consider the following:

- Customer identities

- Customer communication methods

A customer is not limited to mailing and billing addresses and a phone number. Today, almost everyone has a smartphone. New technologies have also added many electronic identities to the physical one. We have one or more e-mail addresses and many social media identities. It could also make sense to add the virtual identities people use in chat rooms and games as well as their virtual life identities.

With all these identities comes many new ways to understand and interact with customers. The two main new communication mediums we'll focus on are smartphones and social media.

Smartphones

A smartphone is by definition a communication device. It can connect to the Internet through the provider's telecommunication network or through a Wi-Fi connection. When a user moves around and passes by a Wi-Fi hotspot, the smartphone communicates with the hotspot to get the information so the user can choose to connect to it. Even if the connection is not established, the exchange of information between the smartphone and the hotspot is sufficient to uniquely identify the phone. Then it is an issue of tying the unique phone ID to a customer identity.

Many stores have Wi-Fi, and some make it available for free to their customers. The Wi-Fi can serve to identify a smartphone, and a physical transaction could be used to tie a customer identity—through, let's say, a loyalty program card—to the location of the unknown phone. After a few more such transactions, we can assume with a high level of certainty that that specific phone belongs to this specific customer. This opens the door to all sorts of potential services because a customer can be identified as soon as she enters the store and the business interaction history is available as a guide to help improve the customer experience.

Here is a hypothetical scenario: a regular customer enters a coffee shop. She is detected by the Wi-Fi. The store system tracks her and, just before she gets to the register to place her order, the barista sees a message on her screen providing basic information so she can address the customer by name and ask if she wants her usual. This could be taken further, where once the customer is detected, an SMS message is sent and all the interaction is done in that format and could even include electronic payment. A preference could also be set to decide whether the interaction should be at the register or through SMS messages.

Technologies are currently on the market that provide indoor proximity systems that can allow a smartphone application to interact with the customer when she gets close to the targeted products included in the proximity system. The customer can be informed of rebates and special offers related to the products in her current location.

Efforts are in place to provide targeted marketing to smartphone users based on their location and, in some cases, the time of day. Imagine getting a notification of a special on fried chicken when you are on your way home from work and close to a store. A balance will need to be reached so as to not alienate the customer, but this capability has the potential to completely change the way companies interact with their customers.

Social Media

The different forms of social media available create new customer identities as well as new avenues for interacting with customers and managing brands.

We've all heard about viral videos and trending subjects in social media platforms. This type of exposure can work both ways. It can dramatically raise the popularity of a brand or product, but on the other hand, a problem could snowball into a disaster that could damage a brand for a long time.

It is important to monitor the social media platforms for trends concerning our products, brands, and company. If a buzz develops, we must find out what it's about to see if we can leverage it in some way, even if it is negative. If it is positive, we can find opportunities to generate more business. If it is negative, we must address the issues as quickly as possible and take to the social media to explain what is being done to correct the situation. A well-orchestrated campaign with a genuine resolution can turn a negative sentiment into goodwill toward the company. The result is increased customer loyalty and possibly new customers.

Another aspect of social media and how it relates to customer identities is that it brings into the open a customer's relationship with other people. It also exposes subjects of interest to the customer as well as common interests with different subsets of people. A company can start keeping track of the people in a customer network and the subjects discussed.

One obvious opportunity arises when a competitor's product is mentioned on Twitter by a customer or someone in her network. If she mentions it, this may mean she is interested in the product, which opens the door to offers toward your product. If one of her friends mentions it, an offer to her may lead to a word-of-mouth marketing to the person in the network or through direct advertising to the friend.

We are still in the early days of big data and social media data mining. There are many other ways this data can be used to generate opportunities. It seems to be limited only by our imagination.

Role of Data in Motion

Hopefully this discussion has made it clear that there is a place for data-in-motion processing in the enhanced 360° view of the customer. We need to sift through all the social data for relevant entries. This requires sophisticated text analytics and targeted processing to identify the company's products and related competitors' products. There is the important task of managing brands through the monitoring of buzz and sentiment. These have to be addressed in real time, but also must be kept in a big data repository for further analysis and extraction of additional identities for the company's customers.

IBM has an offering that is part of the InfoSphere BigInsights product that includes these types of capabilities (see Figure 2-1).

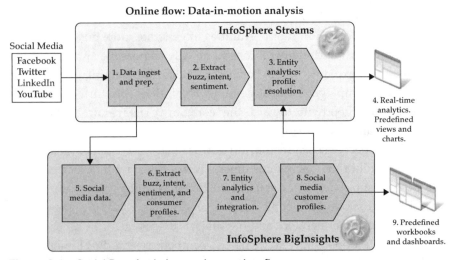

Figure 2-1 *Social Data Analytics accelerator data flow*

This figure is a great example of the synergy between the data-in-motion system (in this case, InfoSphere Streams) and the big data repository (InfoSphere

BigInsights). Of course, this system, being part of the big data architecture, can integrate with other parts that may be required in the enterprise.

Security and Intelligence

Security and intelligence go hand in hand with real-time processing. In fact, the data-in-motion product, InfoSphere Streams, started as a research project between IBM research and the U.S. government to handle these types of issues.

One reason a data-in-motion platform such as InfoSphere Streams is so appropriate is because of the time component of these activities. We all heard about the big U.S. retailer security breach that compromised millions of credit cards. It is a good thing that they discovered the breach. However, it would have been even better to discover and address the breach when it started happening.

Security and intelligence are important to governments and companies alike, especially because the world is so interconnected. Here are some areas where security and intelligence apply:

- **National security**   This includes video surveillance, wire taps, communications, call records, monitoring Internet traffic, identify patterns and relationships among vast information sources, and so on.

- **Infrastructure security**   All the essential services must be protected, including the electricity grid, water resources, and transportation. Because of our interconnected world, this has to cover both physical security[1] and cyber security.

- **Disease/epidemic detection**   Social media can be used to detect the spread of disease.[2] In the case of an epidemic, the sooner it is detected, the quicker it can be brought under control.

- **Company security**   This includes both physical security and cyber security and can include issues such as denial of service attacks, phishing, and malware. We discuss company security in more detail later in the chapter.

- **Fraud detection**   This is a vast subject that we cover in more detail later in the chapter.

Traditional security operations and technology need to be expanded to include a broader data set, as illustrated in Figure 2-2.

Figure 2-2 *Security data set*

For example, by monitoring the network access of employees and machines over time, we can detect changes in the access patterns. An employee sending information to a new host could indicate that the machine is infected with a new virus. This could also apply to point-of-sales systems. If these systems change their usual pattern of network access, this should be detected and investigated right away.

An employee may have access to customer databases, source code, confidential reports, and so on. If the access patterns change to, let's say, a surge of access and download of information to a local computer, it could indicate that the employee is working on a project that requires this type of activity. It could also indicate that the employee is gathering information for other reasons, such as spying for another company or preparing to leave for a competitor. It would be important to investigate these possibilities before the damage is done.

Another interesting security/fraud possibility is to use both the point-of-sale location and the customer location to validate a transaction. This could be done if the customer's cell phone is associated with the customer profile held by the company. If the cell phone is not in proximity of the transaction location, it could raise an alarm, making more verification required to complete the transaction.

Streaming capabilities complement a security solution because it can sift through a lot of data very quickly and do analytics to generate actionable events and help prevent security problems. A product such as InfoSphere Streams takes this a step further because it can take advantage of models developed using historical data to score the streaming data and provide more refined analytics.

Operational Analysis

Operational analysis is basically the analysis of log data produced by the components in an overall business operation that are used to improve the data center operation and produce better business results.

There are multiple sources of data that come in various formats. Some are common to any industry, but others are more specific. Here are two examples of potential data sources and what they produce:

- **Data centers**   Operating system logs, web and application server logs, database logs, network monitoring logs, and so on.

- **Specialized devices**   Smart meters, factory equipment sensors, field sensors, and so on.

Much of the operational data can be analyzed through data-at-rest methods such as IBM InfoSphere BigInsights. However, a time component is still important in many cases. Security concerns is the obvious example, as discussed in the previous section. Still, here is a simple case that shows how crafty some people are and how an ingenious scheme done without malice could still cause a security concern:[3]

A programmer at a telecommunication company hired a contractor in China to do his job based on his scheduled hours. The employee received excellent reviews until one day something alerted the security team of a possible intrusion. It turned out the employee had

FedExed his RSA token to his contractor so he could access the internal system of the telecommunication company. The issue was resolved and no damage was done to the telecommunication company.

This type of creative approach to employment could have caused a major security breach. It is important to stay vigilant and try to detect issues as soon as possible.

One of the key tasks in operational analysis is root-cause analysis. If a system fails, many different logs need to be analyzed and correlated to find out what caused the problem in the first place. Many companies depend on the smooth running of their data center to generate income. In some cases, an hour of downtime means millions of dollars of revenue lost. Finding the root cause of downtime can prevent other service interruptions and improve the company's bottom line.

In some cases, the cause of a service disruption can be fixed by changing some overall characteristics of the system. In other cases, it may not be that straightforward. Analyzing the multiple log sources in real time could provide the needed lead time to avoid the interruption.

Real-time analytics applies to many other areas, including customer interactions. Just look at click stream analytics. Is it possible to change a customer's interactions to guide him into a more successful path that can lead to better customer satisfaction and more company revenues?

Data Warehouse Augmentation

Data warehouse augmentation is definitively a data-at-rest use case. It leverages a landing zone to cleanse and transform the data before loading the data in a data warehouse. The landing zone can also be used for exploration and some querying, thus offloading some of the work from the traditional data warehouse.

Data-in-motion processing could have a small place here, such as preprocessing the data as it arrives to put it in the landing zone. This could be an additional task because it analyzes data to generate real-time actionable alerts.

Internet of Things

We have been hearing about the Internet of Things (IoT) for a few years now. We could look at it as an extension to what IBM defined back in 2005 as a smarter planet: instrumented, interconnected, and intelligent. Wikipedia provides the following definition:

> "The Internet of Things... refers to the interconnection of uniquely identifiable embedded computing-like devices with the existing Internet infrastructure."

It is tempting to dismiss it as a lot of hype and little results; however, the trend is there. Here are some examples:

- *Google acquires Nest lab.* In January 2014, Google paid $3.2 billion to acquire Nest, a maker of networked home monitoring devices.

- *Google acquires Dropcam for $555 million.* Dropcam is a maker of home security devices.

- *GE markets the GE Link smart light bulb.* GE now markets a light bulb that connects to the Internet and can be controlled through an iOS or Android device. Prices start at around $15.

It does not stop there. Here are some titles of articles published in the first half of 2014:

- "Sonar Buoys Help Spot and Recognize Sharks Before It's Too Late"

- "These Parking Meters Know If You're Driving a Gas-Guzzler"

- "Dueling Efforts to Let Connected Devices Talk Will Make It Tough for Them to Talk"

- "These Printed Circuits Could Connect Any Object For Just a Few Cents"

- "Is Your Android Device Telling the World Where You've Been?"

The trend is clear: everything can eventually be connected. Consortiums exist to standardize the communication, so a few standards are being created.

Perhaps the most alarming article is the last one listed, on Android devices. The same problem is currently found in iOS devices, but is apparently being addressed in iOS 8. Still, a lot of personal information can be gathered to help companies better market their products to individuals. The more that can be gathered, the more can be inferred.

The Power of Habits

Most people are creatures of habit. They follow the same (or very similar) routines every day. With GPS-enabled phones, it is easy for companies to track our movement and figure out where we spend our time. Changes in these habits can indicate marketing opportunities.

Some of the data can be collected and analyzed later, but there are situations where if an action is not taken right away, the opportunity of taking action is lost. For example, walking or driving by an area at a specific time of day can provide an opportunity. Early in the morning, it could be an offer on coffee. Around lunch time, it could be the lunch specials at restaurants around a person's location. Late afternoon, the same restaurants could make an offer for take-home food if the data indicates the person is heading home. These are all marketing opportunities that disappear quickly.

What about the connected devices used in a house? By tracking habits, a device's provider can find anomalies that could even lead to sending the police or paramedics if a medical emergency is suspected.

Even medical devices are being developed as connected devices. Google and Novartis are working on contact lenses that can constantly monitor the blood sugar of diabetic people. The development of new connected monitoring devices opens the door to interesting applications. One simple application is better monitoring of health and physical activities. Another is providing a service that monitors health metrics and, using predictive analytics, takes action (for example, contacting the customer to check on her status). This could reach a point where paramedics can be dispatched to address a life-or-death situation as indicated by the health metrics collected. This scenario could be particularly interesting for elderly people who want to continue to live independently as long as possible.

Connected Cars

Modern cars are data centers on wheels. They also provide connectivity as a Wi-Fi hotspot. Most cars have over 1,500 sensors, some of them generating data at millisecond intervals. All that data collection can provide indications on how people drive cars, which car part suffers the most from utilization, how it should be adapted to the real driving conditions, and when to do regular maintenance.

Considering the number of cars sold, we can see that car companies are becoming information companies. The information collected on where the cars are and what they are doing can be useful in many ways (for example, microweather reporting and traffic conditions). The deployment of an airbag would indicate a potential accident. Correlating data from other cars in proximity could confirm the suspicion.

Many cars changing lanes at a specific location could indicate a lane closure, an accident, or debris on the road. Multiple cars turning on their wipers could indicate rain. Figure 2-3 gives some ideas on how different types of data could be generated or used in a connected car ecosystem.

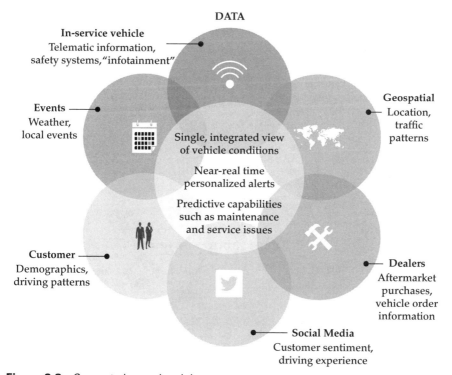

Figure 2-3 *Connected car–related data*

In the few examples presented thus far, we see that there is a need to correlate information coming from multiple sources and provide information in real time so that actions can be taken immediately. For example, this could be in the form of an alert sent to cars in a given area with suggestions on an alternative route to their destination.

Another application of connected cars that may not be obvious in Figure 2-3 is for insurance companies. Information such as miles driven, areas driven in, and other measurements could be used to set insurance rates. In fact, we've already seen some of this starting to be applied with offers such as Progressive Snapshot and other offers based on miles driven per year.

Smarter Cities

Cities need to attract good companies and citizens to continue to survive. They also have to manage their assets efficiently. Figure 2-4 illustrates the multiple aspects that must be addressed for a city to be successful.

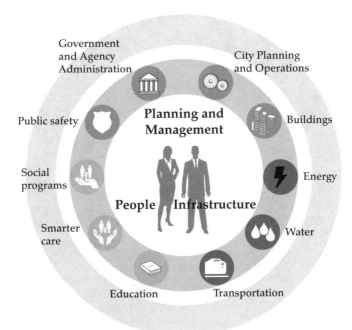

Figure 2-4 *Circle of concerns and influence for smarter cities*

Cities must continue to improve their services and their infrastructures to serve their citizens. Here are some of the most important aspects to consider:

- Reducing congestion in transportation systems

- Reducing crime and improving emergency response

- Improving services, especially in education and training

- Providing efficient access to health care as well as early disease detection and prevention

Traffic causes significant losses in time and money. Improving transportation systems requires planning but also real-time analysis of the current state of the roads. Real-time data can be collected through cameras, GPS systems in public transportation, and city government vehicles. The data needs to be correlated in real time to provide up-to-the-minute alternative routes to reduce the overall congestion.

For example, in Ireland, the Dublin City Council implemented a smarter cities solution to tackle traffic congestion.[4] They implemented a network of sensors with geospatial data for 1,000 buses in real time, enabling traffic controllers to identify and solve the root causes of congestion in the city's bus transport network. This allowed them to see the health of the whole traffic network in real time.

It is easy to see that reducing crime and improving emergency response requires the coordination of multiple systems in real time. Some of the concerns include safety at public events and gang-related activities.

Other Possibilities

Many other possibilities apply to the Internet of Things. In fact, it permeates all industries. The basic components of an IoT solution start with the machine-generated data through sensors in all sorts of devices, including smartphones. The solution also includes all the social data generated by users, mobile or otherwise.

There is a need to analyze and sift through all this data to generate actionable information. A distributed real-time analytics platform is a key component to address this challenge.

Use Cases by Industry

Many use cases apply to multiple industries. For example, many companies have call centers for customer support. We know that information can be retrieved quickly to provide context to the agent so she can better serve the customer. One simple improvement would be to make sure the agent has the appropriate information when she starts interacting with the customer as to not have the customer repeat the same information multiple times. One interesting application to improve on customer satisfaction would be to analyze the conversation in real time, through voice-to-text conversion and text analytics, to provide some guidance on the direction to take. For example, the customer support person could have a dashboard that provides indications of the customer mood and key areas where to lead the conversation, whether that be toward a new product or to apply incentives to improve customer satisfaction. It could also be used as an alert system to get management involved when a call begins to degenerate, so as to provide additional support to solve the situation.

Other situations that apply to multiple industries include machine control (such as in any manufacturing) and data center monitoring. Of course, the big data use cases discussed earlier also apply to many industries.

The following sections provide a sampling of use cases of where InfoSphere Streams can be applied. In many cases, Streams is already used in these areas.

Aerospace and Defense

This section does not go into great detail but instead provides some examples of what is needed in the aerospace and defense industry. Many areas can require data-in-motion support:

- Data analysis for flight tests
- Maintenance, repair, and overhaul of equipment
- Continuous flight operations
- Site security
- Military and national security

Each flight test generates terabytes of data. It is important to be able to sift through and analyze it quickly. Analytics can be applied to detect and predict engine failure, for example. Having a distributed real-time analytics platform can greatly speed up this processing.

Site security is important in all industries but reaches a particular level of concern when it is related to defense. Detecting intrusions can be done using underground fiber optic cables and acoustic data and cameras. We don't want to find out if there was an intrusion; instead, we want to prevent it. Acoustic and video data must be analyzed in real time and generate alerts as early as possible to avoid being compromised. An IBM partner has a security fiber optic solution that is powered by InfoSphere Streams for real-time analytics.

National security requires the analysis of all sorts of data and correlations to arrive at actionable information. This includes flight manifests, telecommunication data, social data, and so on.

When it comes to the military, making the right decision based on accurate information is a matter of life and death. There is data for the operation of the overall installation—whether that be a base or a ship—and there is data related to field operations that can come from radars, satellites, sonars, and so on. The data has to be analyzed in real time, correlated with other pieces of data, and shared with other entities for more efficient response. Figure 2-5 illustrates what an overall maritime solution for defense could look like.

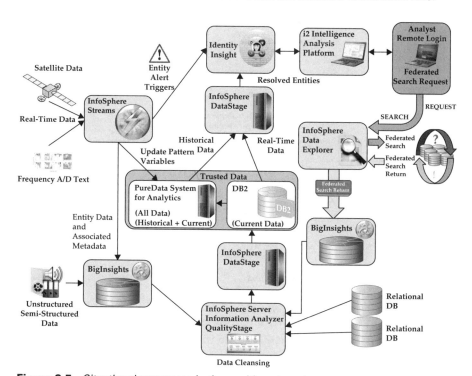

Figure 2-5 *Situational awareness in the maritime domain*

In this figure, we see that a lot of other components are needed to provide a complete system. This is why it is so important that a real-time component fits within a big data architecture. If we focus on the real-time part of Figure 2-5, we see that in this case InfoSphere Streams sifts through the data coming from satellites and other sources. The data is processed, and alerts are generated in real time. The processed data is then stored in a landing zone for further processing.

InfoSphere Streams can also apply scoring based on models developed on the trusted data set. This is the data that was processed from the landing zone and accepted in the official repository. The models running in Streams can be refreshed as needed without interruption to the real-time processing.

Banking

Just like for most industries, there are many areas where big data can be used to improve the banking business. This is illustrated in Figure 2-6.

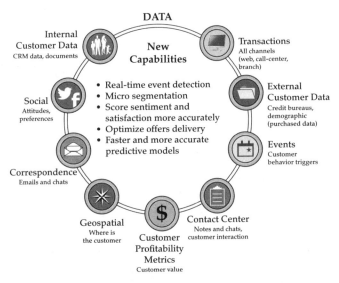

Figure 2-6   *Banking big data capabilities*

Several of these areas include a real-time component. Obviously, the risk and fraud areas are prime candidates. An interesting area is in what is called "sanctioning." Banks execute a large amount of transactions with other financial entities, whether that be companies or individuals. Each of these transactions is subject to regulations where they have to identify these entities so as to not transact with unauthorized ones. Entities such as North Korea, Iran, and Cuba are unauthorized countries; other entities can be terrorist groups or affiliates, for example. The problem with sanctioning is that it can be complicated by misspellings and aliases, among other things. Because the check must be done before the transaction is completed, it has a big impact on the completion of transactions. Unauthorized transactions are subject to significant fines. For example, French bank BNP Paribas agreed to plead guilty to violating U.S. sanctions against Sudan, Cuba, and Iran and paid close to $9 billion in fines.[6] This was a lot more than missed verifications, but it still illustrates the importance of proper verifications.

Oil and Gas

The oil and gas industry has many places where real-time monitoring is needed. For example, all the facilities and pipelines for proper operation and security must be monitored. Another area where real-time monitoring is crucial is oil exploration and production.

An offshore oil platform (oil rig) includes over 40,000 sensors that must be monitored. This may appear to be the primary area of focus for real-time monitoring, but IBM customers in this field have actually focused elsewhere first to get huge benefits.

Moving an oil rig is expensive and takes time. When drilling in the Artic, an operator needs to be constantly on the lookout for ice floes that can threaten an installation. It takes, on average, three days to move an oil rig and another three days to put it back in place. A more accurate prediction of the trajectory of ice floes can reduce the overall window when the oil rig is moved and waiting to be put back in place and results in millions of dollars of additional oil extraction. In some cases, the prediction can indicate that a particular ice floe is not actually a threat and result in even more extraction. The predictions are done in real time using satellite imaging and meteorology and oceanography data. For one specific customer, the savings is estimated at $300 million per season in drilling mobilization costs alone.

The drilling season in the north Atlantic is also impacted by endangered species. The Atlantic cod is labeled as vulnerable and is therefore protected.

It happens that it reproduces during a one-to-two-month period annually. During that time, drilling has to be suspended. By analyzing sonar data, an oil rig operator can detect the presence of fish in real time and more accurately predict the season and thus increase the drilling time.

Electronics

The electronics industry has the same needs as other industries when it comes to sales, marketing, and services. In this area, the same solutions apply in handling big data, whether that be for sentiment analysis, call centers, and so on.

On the production side, a lot of machine data can be analyzed in real time to ensure the proper operation of the equipment by automating preventive and corrective maintenance. There is also the analysis of the results to improve quality. For example, IBM Burlington tests 8.5 billion transistors per day with the help of InfoSphere Streams in the production of the Power processor.

Energy and Utility

Chapter 1 discussed the move from electricity utilities to smart meters, which basically multiply the amount of data collected by a factor of around 3,000. Such an increase in data cannot be followed by a similar increase in processing capabilities and storage. New ways of processing need to be considered to handle the volume and take advantage of the new opportunities this data provides.

Getting data at a faster rate means a better view of overall energy consumption. It also allows for better overall control to reduce peak demand and thus reduce the incidence of brownouts. This can only be done if the data is analyzed quickly to provide an accurate picture of the current state of energy utilization as well as appropriate predictions on how it is changing throughout the day so as to anticipate and resolve potential issues. With the amount of data coming in every 15 minutes (or even quicker), landing the data on disk before the analysis is an extra step that energy companies cannot afford. Continuous analysis that includes the most recent data also lends itself to the distributed real-time analytics model.

The volume of consumer data is just part of the story. Several other aspects need to be considered in the overall smart grid:

- New sources of energy production
- Grid operation
- Security

Energy production is moving to smaller scales. Take, for example, solar energy. Many households are installing solar panels; several large companies are even looking at solar as possibly the only source of energy for some of their installations.[7] There is a surplus of energy at some times of the day that is fed back into the grid. All these new interactions must be managed in real time. We can add to that the electric car, which can change the energy consumption patterns.

The operation of the grid itself generates a large amount of data that is now available due to network connections. It is becoming possible for an energy company to monitor transformers and figure out when to schedule maintenance in order to reduce or eliminate failures. In the case of failures, the problem can now be detected instead of waiting until customers start calling to say they have lost power. The amount of data generated by all the equipment comes at much faster intervals than the smart meters.

There are also concerns about the security of the grid. This includes the physical security of the installations and the security of the computer systems managing the smart grid. These are general real-time monitoring activities we have discussed earlier.

Government

We discussed earlier what can be done with smarter cities and also talked about security in the aerospace and defense sector. Still, there is more that can be done.

The safety of cities also requires constant monitoring. It might start, for example, with sensors at multiple locations, inside and outside, for the detection of gas leaks. Then, there are concerns related to disease detection and prevention that are time sensitive: the sooner a disease is detected, the easier it is to handle. This can include monitoring hospital activities and even tweets indicating some hotspots of illness that could lead, for example, to a specific restaurant. Finding the cause of the illness could lead to actions such as closing a site or even forcing a product recall.

Here are some other areas of concern:

- Monitoring water quality and the spread of chemicals
- Tracking natural disasters
- Early alarm systems for flooding and other natural events

The monitoring of water requires readings and the correlation of multiple sensors in real time to provide proper input to scientists for further analysis.

The tracking of natural disasters such as wildfires requires the analysis of satellite images that can then provide information to where the fire fighters should go next or where they should be deployed to more efficiently get the fire under control.

On the early alarm system front, Ireland's Maritime Institute monitors sensor-equipped buoys to detect floods sooner. It has the additional benefit of monitoring pollution and the state of the local marine life.

Overall, we can see that there are multiple needs for the government to monitor data in real time. The sources of data are varied and plentiful, requiring complex processing to provide quick response.

Healthcare

A lot is being done at IBM in terms of collecting and analyzing data to assist doctors (see IBM Watson cognitive computing). The basis of this data collection is the Watson Foundation, which is basically the big data architecture covered briefly in Chapter 1.

A lot more can be done in terms of monitoring. A good example is in intensive care units (ICUs). The equipment used should be monitored for potential failure, but the data generated by these instruments also needs to be analyzed. There are two main reasons for this:

- Alarm fatigue
- Quicker problem determination

Some ICUs are faced with an average of 350 alarms per day per patient.[8] With the number of patients in an ICU, it is easy to understand that the personnel become desensitized to the alarms. Furthermore, with all these alarms and all the readings on numerous machines, it is very difficult to really know what is going on, and some crucial information is easily missed.

One reason for all these alarms is that these instruments that take measurements on the patient all work in isolation. For this reason, they must have a narrower range of "normal" values. If instead it was possible—and it is—to aggregate all the data, a much better view of the situation could be provided. This real-time correlation work is a great fit for InfoSphere Streams.

The aggregation and correlation of these multiple data sources are crucial at providing a complete picture of the situation. All the separate data points are now available in context and can make discovering trends and problems faster.

This type of approach has been applied in several situations, with benefits such as the following:

- Capturing and analyzing ICU monitor data in real time to alert clinicians and help prevent brain damage

- Predicting rising brain pressure to help prevent higher risk situations

- Predicting critical changes in the patient conditions, providing more time for life-saving medical responses

- Detecting illnesses in newborns up to 24 hours earlier

- Early warning systems that detect subtle signs of atrial fibrillation in patients in the intensive care unit

- Enabling early detection and intervention to mitigate deterioration in a patient's condition

It is easy to see the bottom-line benefits: issues addressed early are easier to resolve and therefore less expensive. In some cases, this can also mean the difference between life and death.

Insurance

Insurance companies have to handle the same customer services and other common business tasks as other companies. For this reason, they have to be concerned with all the changes that have been occurring in mobile devices and social media. They also can augment their customer support with text analytics, as described before. One thing that is particularly important is the management of risk and fraud.

Here are some examples of the activities insurance companies must perform:

- Analyzing all the available data, detecting fraud, and managing risk in real time
- Identifying fraud before a policy is issued
- Identifying fraud before a payment is made
- Developing loss models and applying them in real time

These activities have different real-time requirements. A company that can get an accurate current picture of where it stands can make a better decision on the next best action to take. InfoSphere Streams can play a role in many of these areas and enable companies to achieve their goals.

Telecommunication

Telecommunication companies are at the center of all the big data activities because they enable the connections among all the devices. Their involvement is far reaching. Here are examples of use cases where telecommunication companies can be involved:

- Location-based services
- Cross-industry solutions
- Network/IT infrastructure transformation
- Voice and data fraud
- Network analytics
- Network intelligence
- Proactive call center
- Customer data/location monetization
- Real-time promotion and campaigns (discussed next)
- Social media insight
- Next best action

All these use cases require the real-time analysis of large amounts of data. For example, one Asian telecommunications company uses InfoSphere Streams to process over seven billion call detail records (CDRs) per day.

In some areas of the world, telecommunication companies need to constantly come up with new ways to attract and retain customers. In these regions, customers are not attached to a contract. This means they can switch providers for any reason. Multiple characteristics can indicate that a customer is likely to change her provider. For example, if a customer experiences multiple dropped calls, she may decide to make the switch. The provider must analyze the records, find the issues, correlate with the customer information and history, and decide what should be the next step in making sure the customer is satisfied with the service and does not want to change providers. The response to service issues can range from providing credits to reimburse for the trouble, to offering discounts for a new phone or additional services.

Sprint, a large wireless carrier with over 53 million users, sees the value of InfoSphere Streams for real-time predictive analytics:[9]

> "The goal is to look forward in predictive mode—make adjustments in real time: that's really what we are trying to do from the network side with big data."

Sprint also sees immediate business value:

> "We are going to put real-time intelligence and control back into the network. We are now able to see the transactions, we are able to make minute details and shifts on the data just out the gate. We have had almost a 90% increase in capacity right out of the bag."

IBM is working with many telecommunication carriers around the world to bring them these benefits.

Summary

We started this chapter with some general rules on how real-time processing should be considered. This was followed by a discussion of where InfoSphere Streams distributed real-time analytics processing fits within the IBM five major use cases that apply to all industries.

A big data use case discussion would not be complete without a discussion on the Internet of Things and its far-reaching implications for businesses as well as individuals. The availability of data from all sorts of sensors, as well as the utilization of smartphones, have created a rich set of data that begs to be mined for better tailored services. The possibilities seem limitless; they are only limited by our imagination on how to utilize the data.

The last section of the chapter went through multiple use cases per industry and showed how InfoSphere Streams has been or could be used to benefit the users.

Ultimately, this chapter is about helping the reader unlock her imagination and apply her domain expertise to see how the distributed real-time analytics model could be applied to augment her environment and generate new business opportunities.

Endnotes

1. "Assault on California Power Station Raises Alarms on Potential for Terrorism," http://online.wsj.com/news/articles/SB1000142405270 2304851104579359141941621778

2. "Digital Disease Detection: We See The Trends, But Who Is Actually Sick?" http://healthmap.org/site/diseasedaily/article/digital-disease-detection-we-see-trends-who-actually-sick-62314? utm_campaign=Q3%202014%20Innovation%20Social&utm_ medium=social&utm_source=vector&utm_content=Vector%20 digital%20epidemiology

3. "U.S. programmer outsources own job to China, surfs cat videos," http://edition.cnn.com/2013/01/17/business/us-outsource-job-china/

4. www.ibm.com/midmarket/ie/en/att/pdf/IBM_DCC_130715.pdf

5. http://www.adelosinc.com/

6. http://www.reuters.com/article/2014/07/01/us-bnp-paribas-settlement-idUSKBN0F52HA20140701

7. http://www.bloomberg.com/news/2013-10-24/wal-mart-now-has-more-solar-than-38-u-s-states-drink-.html

8. http://jama.jamanetwork.com/article.aspx?articleid=1696094

9. http://www.youtube.com/watch?v=eg8KSLAZ2HM

3

Program, Framework, or Platform

This chapter explores how we can process data in motion. There are three possibilities:

- **Writing a standalone program** The standalone program is the build-your-own approach using a standard programming language such as C++ or Java.

- **Using a distributed framework** The distributed framework provides the building blocks for distributed processing in the context of a specific programming language.

- **Using a specialized platform** The platform is a superset of the previous choices and adds capabilities that make it a more complete environment.

We explore the pros and cons of each approach in implementing a solution that will run a strategic system for the enterprise.

Build Your Own

When you think about it, processing data in motion is the same thing as having a program processing data. It is tempting to think that we could simply write programs from scratch to answer all our needs. The reason why this is not appropriate is better explained through an example.

Let's say you want to process information that comes from a file and then write the result into a database. To make things simple, the file lines are comma delimited, and each represents a row to store in the database. This is illustrated in Figure 3-1.

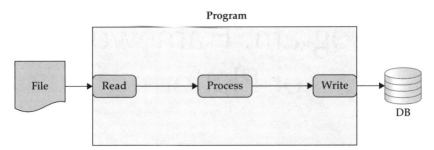

Figure 3-1 *Simple program for reading a file and writing to a database*

This program reads a file one line at a time. It then processes the line, splitting it using a comma as the delimiter into a set of attributes to insert into a database. Once that is done, it executes the INSERT statement and puts the data into the database repository.

That is simple enough. The amount of code required is not large, and we are able to write the program relatively quickly. The problems start appearing when the volume of data increases. We then need more processing power.

Today's computers include multiple processors, and each processor has multiple cores. The simple program illustrated in Figure 3-1 can only use one core from one CPU because it is written as a serial process that is a single processing unit. Most current servers use CPUs with eight cores each, meaning that eight concurrent threads of execution are supported. Our simple program would only use 12.5 percent of one CPU. The resulting solution would experience performance problems as the volume increases, and the server would almost appear to be idle.

To take advantage of all the processing power, we have to either use multiple programs or use a programming technique called multithreading. Therefore, when the volume of data starts putting pressure on the window of time we have allocated to load the data, we can use multiple processors and cores to take advantage of the full power of the machine our program is running on. Keep in mind that loading the data is only a part of the requirements. The entire business process is likely to load the daily data, execute some analytics, create some projections and reports, and so on. Therefore, we cannot take 24 hours to load 24 hours of data. The faster the data is loaded, the quicker we can get to doing the analytics.

In our simple example, the first pressure point is likely to be writing to the database. It is also possible that reading the input file would be faster than the processing of each line into separate attributes. To solve the performance problems, we need to move from a single-threaded program to a multithreaded program, where the three processing elements (reading, processing, and writing) are independent from each other. This way, we can change the number of threads for processing and the number of threads for writing to the database and use as many CPU cores as necessary.

Going to a multithreaded program means that we have independent threads of execution that need to be synchronized in some way. One approach is to use in-memory queues: the reading thread puts the lines on a queue and then the processing threads read the queue and process the lines. They, in turn, put their results on another queue that is then read by database writer threads. This is represented in Figure 3-2.

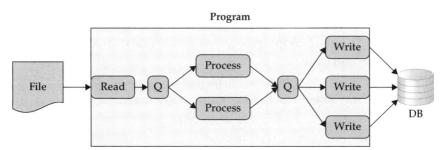

Figure 3-2 *Multithreaded program*

The queue approach is nice because it makes it easier to add threads to address specific bottlenecks. Still, the program now includes quite a bit of additional code to create the queues and process reading and writing to them. It even requires additional code to figure out when all the records are committed to the database after the end of the file has been reached from the input thread.

We started with a simple three-step process, single threaded. However, because of the performance requirements, we ended up writing a significant amount of additional code to provide the infrastructure to support the multithreaded application. In this simple example, the code used to support the multithreaded implementation is likely to be larger than the processing that is done in the single-threaded approach illustrated in Figure 3-1. The code is custom to this specific problem and would have to be reimplemented from scratch for another type of problem.

Remember, we started with maybe the simplest application we could use. A more realistic application would likely have many more steps and much more demanding processing. This can easily lead to a situation where one machine, even with many cores, is not sufficient anymore for the overall processing. In fact, that's the premise behind Hadoop in the case of data-at-rest batch processing. In our case, we simply shift the processing from "at rest" to "in motion."

Moving from a multithreaded program to one that takes advantage of multiple nodes is a major rewrite of the application. We are now dealing with multiple processes and the communication between them. The in-memory queues used in the multithreaded program shown in Figure 3-2 have to be enhanced or replaced. A possible solution is to use message queues. We now have to add a message queue server as well as all the code to read and write to multiple queues. With all the pieces involved—multiple machines, message queue server, multiple processes—we also have to concern ourselves with reliability and availability.

Using a program to process data in motion gives all the flexibility in the world to implement a solution. Still, it is the wrong approach for any sizeable problem because the infrastructure part of the solution would eat the lion's share of resources. The business solution would only use a fraction of the resources required for the implementation. A corporation should focus on its core competency and avoid spending resources in areas outside its expertise.

There has to be a better way to approach these problems so we don't have to reinvent the wheel each time we have new challenges. The next step is to look at getting the distributed processing infrastructure from outside the corporation, learn the API, and focus on solving the business problem. Although this oversimplifies what is required, let's see what this new approach would give us.

Using a Distributed Framework

A distributed processing framework provides the necessary components to implement a distributed computing solution. In our discussion here, we also mean that it is a distributed processing framework specifically for data in motion. There are distributed processing frameworks such as Hadoop that operate in a batch mode on large amount of data. We are talking about a framework for real-time analysis that operates on streaming data. Such a framework includes not only an API to interface with the framework, but also a runtime component that includes capabilities to deploy a program on the cluster and recover from failure.

Because that runtime constitutes the foundation of a solution, it is fair to concern ourselves with its performance: How much overhead does the runtime add? How efficient is the communication layer? What impact do the key features have on the overall performance? Do some features become unusable due to their performance characteristics? How does it scale, not just with more machines, but with more complex processing?

It is beyond the scope of this book to do performance testing and comparison. Just keep in mind that performance and scalability should be a major focus when it comes to the runtime environment.

Over the last few years, a few distributed processing frameworks have appeared on the market. The best-known one is probably the open-source product Storm, now an Apache incubator project. Its major claims are that it is free (open source), easy to use (because it is Java code), and has a community of people contributing to it. We are not here to discuss Storm specifically but rather the fact that frameworks are available to take care of the communication and coordination parts of a stream-processing solution.

Let's look at our previous example, assuming a Java-based framework. The first thing we need to do is write the basic code to read a file. To do that, we would likely use the `FileReader` class to open the file and the `BufferedReader` class to efficiently read the file line by line using the `readLine` method.

The second part of the processing divides each line into its attributes using the comma as a separator. To do so, we need to use the `StringTokenizer` class or the `split()` method and loop over the result until there are no more tokens. We may also then check how many tokens were read and decide if the result is appropriate. There could be additional requirements, such as having a choice when selecting a separator and either ignoring extra fields or generating an error.

The next step involves opening a connection to a database using JDBC. We first load the appropriate class (`Class.forname()` and `DriverManager .getConnection()`) and check for potential errors in case either the class is not found or the connection string is invalid. What is left is to prepare a statement (`prepareStatement()`), bind the values to the proper attributes (`pstmt.setInteger(...)`, for example), execute it (`executeUpdate()`), and check if it completed properly.

All this is expected when writing a program from scratch. The next step is to take care of the distributed part. We have to learn how to use the framework API and add the appropriate code to get the distributed capability of the framework.

These last few paragraphs may have seemed a bit too detailed, but they make a point. Even if you are using a high-level programming language, you still have to worry about all sorts of programming details and the utilization of many APIs. In our case, we used multiple classes along with their specific methods, the framework, and the JDBC APIs, each requiring a significant amount of effort to learn before we can use it in a solution.

Keep in mind that all this has come to light even with the simple application we are using as an example.

APIs are nice because they allow you to interface with all sorts of systems. This could be a new communication system or new processing capabilities. The drawback is that APIs are not standard. You can expect some similarities between APIs for similar types of capabilities, but there is always a big part that is specific to the problem domain. Also, each product will have its own specific characteristics. Therefore, you need to have experts on each API in your development team.

Overall, a distributed processing framework is a big step forward and handles all the distributed processing communication and deployment. It relies on standard programming languages to provide the rest of the capabilities. There are no additional programming constructs specific to the distributed processing of data in motion, and there are limited (or no) specific tools to support the development environment, just the generic programming tooling. As you'll see next, there are more capabilities that can increase productivity.

Using a Streaming Platform

As I said earlier, the performance and scalability of the framework runtime are critical to answer the continuously increasing data-processing needs. This is the basis of a sound solution, but there is a lot more to consider, such as programmer productivity and agility to quickly adjust to changing business needs.

In the old days, you would give a programmer a text editor and a compiler, and this would be enough to get started. We can go one step further and provide a debugger and a source control system. This approach is still in use today, but there are productivity tools available that can make the programmer's life easier. One such tool is an integrated development environment (IDE).

IDE

An IDE provides an environment that includes multiple tools essential to a software environment:

- **Flexible views**   A programmer is interested in viewing multiple things at once when working. This could be the workspace structure, multiple source code files, output of execution, and so on. Depending on the task being performed, this set of views can change. Being able to go from one to the other seamlessly improves the speed of analysis and helps continuity of thought.

- **Text editors**   Text editors usually include programming language syntax recognition. They provide instant feedback on syntax issues and can also include pop-up tips and code-completion capabilities. When appropriate, the IDE could include visual editors to facilitate the building of distributed processing applications.

- **Build support**   As software systems become more complex, there is a need to automate the build process and keep track of the dependencies between modules. The IDE automates this process and ensures that everything is built properly.

- **Execution support**   An IDE provides the ability to look at the result of an execution. It can also include integration with a debugger, which makes it easier to pinpoint and solve issues and get to a deliverable faster.

Obviously, many tools can be used to answer the different programmers' needs, but having an integrated environment makes a platform easier to set up and use, thus making programmers more productive.

Toolkits

Some tasks are commonly done in every program. This is why programming languages such as C come with libraries of functions for programmers to use. A similar approach is used in an object-oriented programming language such as Java, which comes with libraries of classes to address the common tasks such as manipulating strings, manipulating date and time, process grouping of data in arrays and lists, and so on. It also includes more complex class packages to address communicating over a network and talk to a database in the form of additional APIs.

Developing a distributed processing solution for real-time analytics is different from writing a "standard" program. Our target environment is a cluster of machines, so the processing has to run so as to take advantage of as many cores and machines in the cluster as possible. To do this, the overall processing is decomposed in smaller components that we call *operators*. These operators may run as separate threads, separate processes on the same machine, or separate processes running on separate machines.

This operator approach lends itself to a different type of prebuilt capabilities that is different from class libraries. It is similar to going from a third-generation language to a fourth-generation language: it raises the level of programming abstraction just like going from assembler to Fortran/ Cobol/C raises it and going from them to object-oriented languages does the same. Let's call this higher-level set of prebuilt capabilities a *toolkit*. A toolkit would consist of a set of operators that address a specific problem domain. For example, the operators used for the analysis of time-based data can be grouped into a time series toolkit. The operators provided in a toolkit would offer a division of processing that can then be scheduled to run as separate threads or separate processes on the same or different machine.

The availability of operator toolkits provides multiple benefits:

- **High-level capability**   A toolkit provides a set of prebuilt capabilities that doesn't need to be re-created for every project. A programmer simply uses the operator and moves on to the next transformation.

- **Predefined division of labor**   Using prebuilt operators automatically divides your problem into pieces that can take advantage of multiple cores and multiple machines. These operators are also a good example of the average work an operator should do. There are no set rules, but it helps in seeing how the processing should be divided to take advantage of the processing distribution.

- **Standardization**   Earlier I mentioned that with multiple APIs, the programmer is forced to learn a new environment for each API. It is almost like learning a new language each time there is a new API. Using operators moves the level of abstraction higher. The use of parameters to adjust the processing is much easier to understand than how to orchestrate a bunch of API calls. For example, the programmer may want to read a file. A file reader operator can have a set of parameters that allow the programmer to identify the file, provide information such as the separator used in a comma-separated values (CSV) file, and so on. The programmer does not have to worry about how to open the file, use buffering, and other lower-level tasks.

The richer the set of operators provided, the more productive the programmer. Just like we would not accept an object-oriented programming language that does not come with a comprehensive set of classes, a platform for real-time distributed analytics must come with a comprehensive set of operators.

Programming Constructs

This section brings up a few concerns that should be addressed by the programming environment. By doing so, the platform makes programmers more productive, reduces programming errors, reduces the amount of code written, and improves code maintenance.

We limit this discussion to three essential aspects:

- Program modularity capabilities
- Windowing for streaming data
- Executable programs modularity

Program Modularity

The operators give us a higher level of abstraction. We still need to be able to group operators together to perform a specific task. Just like in standard programming, we may need to do the same task in multiple places in the overall processing. Duplicating the code would make it harder to maintain and would be error prone because changes in one copy could be missing in another, thus leading to different behavior in different areas of the overall processing.

A platform programming environment should have the ability to group multiple operators together as one logical unit that can be reused in multiple stages of the processing. This should go as far as providing parameters to the logical unit to modify the processing to fit the specific instance of an operator group.

Windowing

When a program asks a database for an average on a data set, this data set is fixed and finite for the specified query duration. Data in motion does not have a fixed data set. Instead, it represents a stream of data that has no beginning and no end. Any time we need to look at data as a group, we must collect the data for the desired time interval (a window) and then process it.

The platform should include facilities to manage the window of data and provide capabilities to define such things as the window definition, including time interval and count, and additional processing characteristics so programmers don't have to constantly re-create these capabilities.

Executable Modularity

When we are processing data in motion, we are processing unending streams of data. What if we want to add new data sources to our processing or add new types of processing on existing data sources? The platform should provide the ability to accommodate these requirements without application downtime. This can be done in multiple ways, but it starts with the ability to modularize the application so modules can be added to and removed from the overall execution and have the ability to connect to the current flow of data. It could go as far as providing ways to temporarily suspend the flow of data so as to not miss any records.

Extensibility

No platform can answer all the needs of all the users. This is a lesson that has been learned by the computer industry because many products have the ability to add features. You can see forms of extensibility as far back as the software products for the IBM 360 Mainframe, if not earlier. These software products included something called "user exits," which allowed customers to add their own manipulations at different stages of the processing. This concept has evolved where today many products provide much more flexible extensibility capabilities. Just look at database products and IDEs such as Eclipse.

A data-in-motion platform has to be extensible because it is a programming platform. Creating a solution is not just stringing together a set of existing operators. It also involves creating new ones. The extensibility has to support ways to extend the concept of data type and make it as easy as possible to create new operators. The creation of new operators also has to support the use of existing APIs in languages such as C++ and Java.

The Eclipse IDE is the most popular platform in the Unix/Linux environment. A big part of its success is due to the ability to add capabilities to the IDE through plug-ins. A data-in-motion platform has to accommodate extensibility to ensure it answers the needs of its users.

Monitoring Tools

Up to this point we've only talked about the creation of a solution. Eventually, this solution is put in production and needs to be managed. A platform should include a set of tools to manage and monitor running applications. Both GUI-based and command-line-based tools are needed. The former is great as an easy-to-use interactive tool. The latter is essential to help system managers automate some of the management processes. With such tools, a system administrator can ensure that the system is healthy and the application is running, as well as monitor the performance of the components to see how the overall performance could be improved.

Summary

A distributed solution has to take into account multiple cores and multiple machines. It has to have the flexibility to adjust based on changes to the cluster. This is not part of the core competency of most enterprises. The enterprise has to focus on solving its business problems and continue to be competitive in its market. An enterprise should not start from scratch when developing a distributed real-time analytics solution.

Developing a solution can be done in many ways. It has been proven that using higher-level programming languages provides orders-of-magnitude better productivity. A distributed real-time processing solution requires new language constructs to elevate the level of abstraction, just like when going from binary code to assembler, to procedural languages and to object-oriented languages. These new language constructs have to be supported with a set of programmer productivity tools. This is why a complete platform is required.

The need for distributed real-time processing will only increase, and enterprises will continuously need to adapt to changing requirements. Having a platform that optimizes programmer productivity and facilitates runtime management is essential to the competitiveness of an enterprise.

4

InfoSphere Streams

Up to this point, we've talked about the differences between data at rest and data in motion, looked at examples of where data in motion can be used, and discussed why we should use a platform instead of a framework, let alone writing something from scratch. This chapter describes InfoSphere Streams. The goal is not to describe how to use Streams. For that, you can look at the many resources mentioned in Chapter 6 and at the end of the book. Instead, we want to find out what its capabilities are so we can better understand how to apply this technology to our business problems and get to a solution faster. Understanding what a product can do is essential in any discussion of its use in a solution. It is not an issue of how to do something, but rather what can be done. Any nonprogrammer interested in Streams will benefit from this chapter.

After providing a quick background on the origin of the product, this chapter covers five main topics:

- **Runtime** The runtime is the execution part of the product. InfoSphere Streams was created with performance and scalability in mind. We discuss this subject in the "Streams Runtime" section.

- **Language** InfoSphere Streams includes its own language called Streams Programming Language (SPL). This is needed to provided that higher level of abstraction mentioned in Chapter 3. This section also covers the capabilities available in the creation of new operators.

- **Toolkits and accelerators** In Chapter 3, we talked about the need for prebuilt capabilities to improve programmer productivity. The "Streams Toolkits" and "Streams Accelerators" sections cover these capabilities.

- **Development tooling** The "Streams Development Environment" section discusses the capabilities provided in the Streams Studio IDE.

- **Installation and administration** The chapter would not be complete without looking at installation and administration. The "Streams Installation" and "Streams Administration" sections provide a brief overview of the tooling available for this purpose.

InfoSphere Streams Background

InfoSphere Streams started back in 2003 as a joint research project between IBM research and the U.S. government. The goal was to develop a platform that would provide performance and scalability in the real-time analytics of any type of data. These basic requirements were at the core of the InfoSphere Streams design. Additionally, the U.S. government wanted InfoSphere Streams to become a commercially available product. They did not want to get in the business of maintaining the code themselves. Instead, they wanted to focus on their core problem—analyzing in real time a huge amount of data in various formats: structured, semi-structured, and unstructured. Since then, InfoSphere Streams has been through the following commercial releases:

- **Version 1.2.0** February 2010

- **Version 1.2.1** October 2010

- **Version 2.0** April 2011

- **Version 3.0** November 2012

- **Version 3.1** April 2013

- **Version 3.2** October 2013

- **Version 3.2.1** April 2014

At this point, InfoSphere Streams is a mature product in the sense that it has proven to be solid and stable. It has met its goals of performance and scalability. Each new release brings new features that improve the product in many aspects, including performance, scalability, ease of use, ease of development, and ease of installation and administration.

Streams Runtime

Before discussing the runtime environment of InfoSphere Streams, let's take a quick look at the hardware and software platform requirements.

InfoSphere Streams runs under the Linux operating system. It currently supports Red Hat (RHEL), CentOS, and SUSE (SLES). The hardware platforms supported are x86_64 and IBM POWER7 systems.[1] Table 4-1 summarizes the supported mix of operating systems and platforms.

Operating System	System Hardware and Architecture	Supported OS Versions
RHEL	X86_64 (64 bit)	Version 5.6 or later
		Version 6.1 or later
	IBM Power 7 (64 bit)	Version 6.2 or later
CentOS	X86_64 (64 bit)	Version 5.6 or later
		Version 6.1 or later
SLES	X86_64 (64 bit)	Version 11.2 or later

Table 4-1 *Streams Platform Dependencies*

In terms of network connectivity, InfoSphere Streams supports Ethernet and InfiniBand.

InfoSphere Streams is a platform for distributed processing. It can support a large number of machines (cluster) working together to solve a given problem. For this purpose, the runtime environment has to handle tasks such as the following:

- **Security** Any operation on a Streams cluster must be authenticated to ensure that the user requesting a specific service is authorized to do so. Streams supports Pluggable Authentication Module (PAM) and LDAP. It also supports Security-Enhanced Linux (SELinux) for people who prefer that environment.

- **Services location** With potentially hundreds of nodes in the cluster, there is a need to locate distributed services in the instance so the components can communicate with each other. This requires some sort of name services that can provide location-independent communication to all the components.

- **Scheduling**   An application job is made up of multiple operators. When a job is started, Streams must decide where to execute each operator based on the available nodes and their utilization, as well as based on hints that can be provided as part of an operator definition or invocation.

- **High availability and recovery**   With many nodes part of the cluster, there are more chances of failures of all sorts. Streams nodes can be identified as either application nodes, administrative nodes, or mixed nodes. This means that a node can be dedicated to running application operators, dedicated to running administrative services, or available to run both administrative processes and application operators. What happens if a node fails? Administrative nodes need to be restarted and their state recovered. What about application operators? Should they be restarted? These capabilities are part of InfoSphere Streams. Restarting application operators is a configuration decision made by the developer.

This short description gives you an idea of what InfoSphere Streams has to contend with. The efficiency of all these services has an impact on the overall performance and scalability of a cluster. InfoSphere Streams was designed from the ground up to ensure minimal overhead and maximum performance.

A Streams application is basically a directed graph where data flows from operator to operator. The data comes in discrete units called *tuples*. Each tuple is made up of one or more attributes. This is similar in concept to the definition of a row in a relational table or elements in a C structure. As tuples flow through the graph, they go through transformations that are dictated by the specific operator.

An *operator* is a processing thread that has zero or more input ports and emits tuples over zero or more output ports. A *port* is simply an entry point into the operator. There may be multiple streams connecting to a single port as long as they have the same tuple structure.

An operator that does not have any input port is a source operator that generates data itself either through an artificial method or by connecting to a message queue, database, file, and so on. Such an operator that interfaces with the outside world (outside of Streams) is called an *adapter*.

An operator that does not have output ports is considered a sink operator. It writes to output such as files, message queues, and databases.

The ability to have a number of input ports opens the door to the use of control information that can initiate additional processing in an operator, such as reloading an analytics model or refreshing a lookup table.

Figure 4-1 illustrates a simple Streams application.

Figure 4-1   *Simple Streams job graph*

This graph reads tuples from a comma-separated value (CSV) file, filters the tuples based on a condition, and writes the tuples that meet that condition to an output file.

Of course, this is a contrived example of the use of distributed real-time analytics, but it still illustrates the decomposition of the processing into three separate execution units (operators) and the flow of data tuples between these operators.

Here is an example of what the source code for the `FileSource_1` operator could look like:

```
stream<LocationType> FileSource_1  = FileSource()
{
      param
            format : csv ;
            file : "/home/streamsadmin/data/all.cars" ;
}
```

The first line shows that we are using a `FileSource` operator as a source of tuples. We name that instance `FileSource_1`. This operator returns tuples of type `LocationType`, which is a user-defined type. We name the resulting stream `Observations`.

The content of this specific instance of the `FileSource` operator only includes a few parameters. One is used to identify the format of the input file as containing comma-separated values. The second parameter is the path of the file to process. This is all it takes in this case to get this part of the processing done. There are many situations where setting a few parameters is all that is needed to process data through the operators provided with InfoSphere Streams.

Having three separate operators means we could use three separate CPU cores wherever they may be in the cluster. So, how do you start a Streams application job?

A Streams application includes all the information about the separate operators. It is submitted to the Streams instance through a simple utility called streamtool. This utility interacts with the instance services, such as the application manager, the resource manager, and the scheduler. All the communication is transparent to the user submitting the job, making it easy to manage applications, as you will see later in this chapter.

The Streams Processing Language

In Chapter 3, we mentioned the need to use a higher level of abstraction to increase the programmer's productivity. The example of an application job as a directed graph illustrates that there are ways to raise that abstraction level and make it easier to get to a solution.

Traditional languages such as C++ and Java do not have a notion of distributed processing beyond multithreading. SPL answers this need. With SPL, you can think about a solution as a flow of data:

- *Where does my data come from?* Are you reading the data from files, network connections, message queues, databases, and so on? Which operators are needed to acquire that data?

- *What part of the data do I need to process?* Once you have a tuple, is it worth keeping or should it be discarded? Do you need all the attributes of the tuple or should you eliminate some that are uninteresting?

- *Which transformation do I need to perform on my data?* Do you need to convert it for different parts of the processing? What new type of information is required from this data? Do you need to aggregate multiple tuples into averages, trends, and so on?

- *Where do I need to send the data?* Which business process needs that data? It could be multiple business processes, depending on the purpose of your business application.

- *Where do I need to deliver the final results?* It could need to go to a file, a database, a message queue, or an interactive dashboard. Depending on where the data is delivered, the format may also be affected.

Working at this level makes it easier to look at the business processing as a whole and decompose it at a high level into manageable components that can be assigned to different members of a team. It also opens the door to new tooling that allows the manipulation of operators through a graphical editor.

Punctuations

In addition to being able to process data, Streams allows the programmer to add control data to a stream in what is called a *punctuation*. Punctuations can be useful as signals for reloading some lookup tables, identifying an end of a file, dividing the data in groups of tuples, and so on. This is an added flexibility that is specific to a streaming-aware language. Punctuations serve a vital purpose in stream processing that could be difficult to emulate without it.

Windowing

As mentioned in Chapter 3, processing streaming data (data in motion) is different from processing data at rest. A stream of data theoretically has no beginning and no end. Any grouping of tuples needs to be defined. InfoSphere Streams provides a flexible way to define grouping based on criteria such as count, time, and delta. A *delta* is the difference in value of a given attribute from the oldest and the newest tuple in the window.

InfoSphere Streams also supports either a *tumbling window,* which is processed and emptied when the grouping condition is met, or a *sliding window,* which defines separately the condition where tuples are removed from the window and the condition triggering the operation on the tuples in the window.

Having this capability removes the burden from the programmer and makes development more efficient.

Data of All Types

One of InfoSphere Streams' original requirements was to be able to process data of all sorts: structured, semi-structured, and unstructured. The implication was also that data such as sound, images, and videos could be processed. This requires a bit of explanation.

An example of structured data is a row in a database. The row is divided into columns. Each column has a name and holds data of a specific type. For example, consider the following partial relational table definition:

```
CREATE TABLE customer (
    customer_num      int not null,
    firstname         char(15),
    lastname          char(15),
    company           char(20),
    . . .
);
```

The operator reading this database table would create tuples with corresponding attributes that would have a definition like this one:

```
type customer = tuple<int32 customer_num,
                rstring firstname,
                rstring lastname,
                rstring company,
                . . .>;
```

Without understanding the exact syntax here, it is obvious that the tuples generated are structured. This way, operators down the line know about all the attributes and their data types.

A semi-structure input could come in the form of an XML or JSON document. These types of documents are unstructured, but they follow an internal convention that allows a computer program to extract structured information from them.

From a Streams point of view, we would read a data source that provides, let's say, JSON documents. This means the source operator generates tuples containing only one attribute, a character string:

```
type jsondoc = tuple<rstring content>;
```

This is, in fact, no different from reading an unstructured document. The difference is what we do with it. With the JSON document, we can extract specific fields and convert them into structured data. This is done through well-known utilities that know how to parse JSON and extract fields.

So, no matter what, our tuples need to include at least one attribute that then gives access to the data, be it semi-structured or unstructured. What about binary data such as sound, images, and videos?

These pieces of data must be contained in a tuple attribute. Consider a video, for example. It is likely to come in tuples containing a segment of time (say, one hour). Despite being considered unstructured data, a video actually follows a specific convention dictated by one of multiple available standards. It could be subdivided further into smaller segments all the way down to a single image. A similar decomposition applies to acoustic data where the adapter reads a tuple that contains a number of seconds of that acoustic data. It can be decomposed as needed into shorter segments. There are standards for the other types of unstructured data, so the overall structured/ unstructured discussion is a bit muddled.

To receive an unstructured binary type, InfoSphere Streams provides the blob type. Once we have the data, we have to use an appropriate operator that knows how to process it. At the time of this writing, this operator would likely come from either an open-source toolkit or from our own implementation. We discuss toolkits later in this chapter.

When working with unstructured data, we will likely also have structured metadata with it. For example, if we are processing an image, additional information about its origin is likely to be included. This means that our resulting tuple would include attributes for structured data and an additional attribute containing the image. Depending on the type of image provided, one of the first steps in the processing could end up being adding attributes such as image size and geolocation to the metadata.

Several data types are available in InfoSphere Streams. Figure 4-2 shows the data type hierarchy.

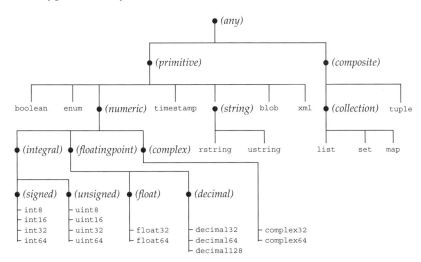

Figure 4-2 *InfoSphere Streams' available data types*

Expression Language

SPL is a streaming language that gives us the level of abstraction needed to work with directed graphs. Still, there is a need for a traditional imperative, functional, or expression language. Note that these are the terms used in the documentation. I prefer *procedural* language.

There is no reason to come up with a brand-new implementation of a procedural language. InfoSphere Streams uses a language closely related to C/C++, with some processing flavors found in common scripting languages. Because of that, learning the SPL expression language requires a very short learning curve for any experienced programmer. One difference is explicit casting, which forces the programmer to identify any type conversions in the code. This reduces potential errors and is one of the features that allows for more optimal compilation, thus leading to better performance.

Writing Operators

As you'll see in the next section, InfoSphere Streams comes with a set of toolkits that define data types, functions, and operators. The set of operators available with the product cannot cover all the needs of all people. Streams is extensible. It is possible to write your own operators by using SPL, Java, or C++. It is beyond the scope of this book to go into this in detail; just know that it is possible. We'll come back to this topic briefly in the section on the development environment.

Streams Toolkits

InfoSphere Streams comes with prebuilt functionality in packaging called toolkits. Furthermore, a substantial set of additional toolkits is available free of charge, hosted on the GitHub site.

A toolkit may include data types, functions, and operators. It represents a logical grouping of functionality designed to address a specific problem domain. InfoSphere Streams comes with the following toolkits:

Standard	Big Data	Complex Event Processing
Database	Financial Services	Geospatial
DataStage Integration	Internet	Messaging
Mining	R-project	Rules
Text	TimeSeries	

The toolkits are continuously being updated, and new toolkits appear in the product from time to time. Other products, such as IBM SPSS, include their own toolkit for InfoSphere Streams integration.

Note that the first toolkit mentioned in the table is the standard toolkit, and it has a special status. It is automatically included in any application. This is because it contains commonly used operators that are considered essential to any application. The other toolkits must be explicitly included in a project to be used—there is no reason to add extra code to a project if it will not be used. The same concept is found in other languages. For example, Java uses the `import` command to add a reference to a specific class. The addition of toolkits to a project also has an impact in the development environment facilities, as you'll see later.

The next several sections highlight some of the available toolkits at different levels of detail to give you an idea of the capabilities provided.

The Standard Toolkit

The standard toolkit includes 38 operators divided into the following categories:

- **Adapter (10)**   These operators provide connectivity to common input/output sources such as files and UDP/TCP network protocols. It can also scan a directory for new content at specific intervals.

- **Relational (6)**   This category includes operators for filtering, converting, sorting, aggregating, and joining. Note that the `Aggregate`, `Sort`, and `Join` operators use the windowing concept mentioned earlier. There is also an operator used to insert punctuation into the data stream.

- **Utility (19)**   This category offers a variety of operators, including some to control the tuple flow. One operator worth mentioning here is the `Custom` operator. `Custom` is basically a blank canvas that allows you to do any processing. It is so powerful that inexperienced people have a tendency to see all operations in a Streams-directed graph as candidates for the use of the `Custom` operator. It is a great way to create your own operators, as long as you don't abuse it and use it to the detriment of the other provided operators in all the toolkits.

- **XML (1)**   The `XMLParse` operator generates tuples from the content of an input XML document.

- **Compat (2)**   Operators provided for compatibility with a much earlier version of InfoSphere Streams.

Many of these operators are found in virtually all Streams projects.

The Big Data Toolkit

The Big Data toolkit includes eight operators used for integration with IBM BigInsights and other Hadoop distributions, as well as with the IBM Watson Explorer product. This is discussed further in Chapter 5.

The Database Toolkit

The Database toolkit has nine operators to provide I/O capabilities with database products, including DB2, Informix, Netezza, SolidDB, MySQL, Oracle, SQL Server, Teradata, and more. It can even use the BigInsights Big SQL interface to access the BigInsights data store through SQL statements.

The Geospatial Toolkit

Geospatial information is now crucial to most big data projects. The Geospatial toolkit provides the capability to manipulate this type of data. It does not include any operators. Instead, it includes 6 conversion functions, 22 geospatial functions, and 10 data types that can be used in operators to manipulate spatial data.

The Internet and Messaging Toolkits

These toolkits provide seven operators to communicate through the following protocols: HTTP, HTTPS, RSS through HTTP/HTTPS, FTP, and FTPS. On the messaging side, the operators support IBM WebSphere MQ, Apache Active MQ, and the MQ Telemetry Transport (MQTT).

The Text Toolkit

A lot of the data generated today is unstructured in the form of free-flowing text. The most prominent example is social media analysis. InfoSphere

Streams shares a common high-level language for text analytics with IBM BigInsights. The language is called AQL, which stands for Annotation Query Language. Streams also uses the same tooling as BigInsights for the creation of text extractors. Note that IBM Watson Explorer, which is part of the IBM big data architecture, also supports AQL as a way to query unstructured data. This discussion also ties in with the accelerators that we cover later in this chapter.

AQL is a declarative language that has a lot of similarities with SQL. This makes it easier to understand because most developers are familiar with SQL. The basic idea is to create declarations similar to SQL SELECT statements and join them together to get the intersection of all the statements involved as the final result. Just like SQL, AQL has an optimizer that looks at query plans to figure out the optimal way to process the query and get to the final answer.

AQL also comes with a few prebuilt extractors that can be used by other extractors. For example, you can use the following AQL code to extract the names of corporations:

```
module MyModule;
import view Organization from module
     BigInsightsExtractorsExport as Organization;
create view GetCorp as
  select GetText(O.organization) as corp
  from Organization O
  group by GetText(O.organization);
output view GetCorp;
```

Assuming that this piece of code is in a file, the module statement identifies which module the file belongs to. The import statement identifies a prebuilt extractor and names it Organization. This is followed by the create view statement, which simply defines a processing view over the document generated by the Organization view. In turn, the Organization view uses the document that it receives as an argument. Finally, the output statement "materializes" the view. At this point, the AQL optimizer looks at the components of the output and figures out the best way to get the result.

A view can get information from any number of other views. It is similar to an SQL view, where the included SELECT statement joins multiple tables together and defines which columns will be part of the result.

During the processing of free text, a word could be ambiguous. Words can have different meanings based on how they are used. Consider the following sentences:

"The problem was solved within a *minute* of the call."
"The problem was solved with a few *minute* adjustments to the environment."

In the first sentence, *minute* is a unit of time; in the second, it is an adjective. Many words have multiple meanings based on their type. AQL includes a feature called part-of-speech that identifies the type of a word. With this feature, it is possible to differentiate between the multiple meanings and get to a more accurate analysis.

AQL includes many additional features. For example, you can define regular expressions, dictionaries, and process the data using any of the many functions available. It is even extensible, so you can add your own function to better fit your business requirements. AQL deserves a book of its own. Hopefully we'll see such a book in the future. We'll talk a bit more about text analytics in the "Streams Accelerators" section.

The TimeSeries Toolkit

The TimeSeries toolkit gives the impression of being specialized for problems in signal processing and seems more appropriate for audio; image, and video signal processing such as processing sonar, EKG, and audio. It is true that this toolkit applies to signal processing, but its capabilities are generic enough to apply to other disciplines. The same methods of linear regressions, interpolation, and extrapolation, just to name a few, can be useful in the processing of any type of time-based data.

The TimeSeries toolkit is divided into four main processing sections: generation, pre-processing, analysis, and modeling. Here are their roles:

- **Generation**   Generates time series for test and validation.

- **Preprocessing**   Prepares data for further processing. This includes calculating missing values, changing the sampling rate to fit the planned processing, and grouping data for further processing.

- **Analysis**   Computes various information about the data. This includes detecting trends, correlating multiple time series and finding patterns, normalizing the data so multiple time series of different scales can be compared, reducing noise in the data, and so on.

- **Modeling**   Uses a range of modeling approaches to predict future values of time series.

Reducing noise may seem like a very specialized processing that has no applicability to business data. However, you can look at reducing noise as a way of reducing the impact of large variations in data readings. Reducing noise and predicting future values involve specific Stochastic methods that are beyond the scope of this book. As a simple example that can be accomplished with the DSPFilter operator low-pass filter capabilities, you can create a moving average to remove short-term variations to reveal the variations that occur on a more meaningful time scale. This method uses the average of a number of recent values. As the values arrive, older values are discarded to create a new average. This is a basic method used in stock analysis, where 5-day and 21-day moving averages are used to get a better picture of the trend of a specific stock. A similar method could be applied, for example, to network load readings to detect a trend and even anticipate when an upgrade should be done.

Open-Source Toolkits

The IBMStreams section on the github.com site includes InfoSphere Streams–related tutorials, demos, sample code, and toolkits. In all, there are 22 sections on different subjects. The toolkits come in source format and are available for free. The GitHub Streams section is continuously changing. Here are some of the most notable toolkits available at the time of this writing (in no particular order):

- **streamsx.hbase**   Provides operators for accessing an HBase data repository.

- **resourceManagers**   At this time, this directory includes the code to support YARN as a resource manager for Streams.

- **Streamsx.json**   Provides an operator that converts a JSON document into structured information based on the parameters provided.

Another site called Streams Exchange hosts some toolkits that will eventually move to the GitHub site. Still, Streams Exchange currently includes some interesting toolkits; one of them is the OpenCV toolkit for image and video processing.

Streams Accelerators

Streams' toolkits speed up development so businesses can get to running their solutions faster. The IBM Big Data development team has taken things one step further with what it calls *accelerators,* which are development templates that provide a solution framework for a specific problem. Here are the accelerators currently available:

- Accelerator for Machine Data Analytics (MDA)
- Accelerator for Social Data Analytics (SDA)
- Accelerator for Telecommunications Event Data Analytics (TEDA)

Of the three, only TEDA is specific to InfoSphere Streams. The SDA accelerator uses a mix of IBM BigInsights and Streams. This section highlights the capabilities of these two accelerators.

Telecommunications Event Data Analytics

The TEDA accelerator provides a solution framework for telecommunications companies for their processing of call detail records (CDRs). Figure 4-3 shows a simplified diagram of the overall solution.

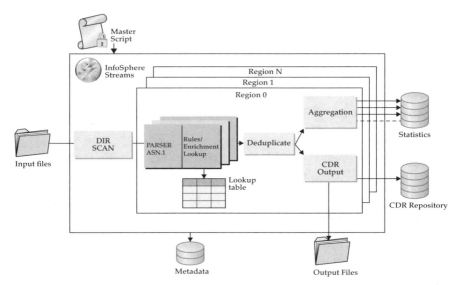

Figure 4-3 *TEDA accelerator architecture*

As input files arrive, they are sent to a parser that understands their specific format, and data is extracted and enriched through the process. Figure 4-3 shows a deduplication step. This process is quite demanding because CDR duplicates can come in quite a few hours after the first one. Eventually, statistics are generated and stored in a repository in addition to the CDRs.

The TEDA accelerator has the following areas of customization:

- **Parser**   TEDA comes with a sample ASN.1 parser and a parser generator. ASN.1 stands for Abstract Syntax Notation One. ASN.1 is a joint standard from three international standards organizations. It defines an abstract syntax of the data to be encoded. Still, because there are many data variations in different companies, users of this accelerator are expected to write their own parser definition and can use the provided parser generator to create the executable.

- **Rule framework**   This framework allows the users to define rules on how to process the tuples (CDRs) and uses them to generate the appropriate SPL code. The framework supports attribute manipulation and simple lookup.

- **Configuration parameters**   Multiple configuration parameters allow the user to tailor the TEDA framework to the number of nodes, number of logical (geographical) regions that should be used, level of parallelism, and so on.

The TEDA accelerator is a specialized framework that has a learning curve. Ideally, a customer would also use IBM services to speed up going from a design to a production solution.

Social Data Analytics Accelerator

Social media cannot be ignored anymore. Companies must pay attention to it, if only for brand protection. If a negative conversation is started on a company's offering, that company must take immediate action to minimize the damage. Left to itself, this situation could turn into a major problem that could hurt the company. A prompt answer to any problem or concern can turn a negative situation into goodwill toward the company.

The Social Data Analytics accelerator provides a platform to address the concerns of optimizing the use of social data.[2] It uses a mix of InfoSphere Streams and InfoSphere BigInsights to provide real-time analytics, as well as further capabilities such as profile reconciliation that require analytics on historical data. Figure 4-4 shows the high-level architecture of SDA.

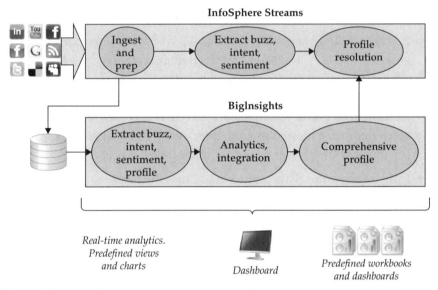

Figure 4-4   *Social Data Analytics accelerator architecture*

The data is ingested through Streams. SDA supports two products that provide access to social data: Gnip and Boardreader. As Streams ingests the data, it also writes that data to BigInsights and moves on to real-time analytics to extract buzz, intent, and sentiment. It can then tie the results to profiles as needed.

BigInsights does a similar type of processing, but also reconciles the different identities of the people on social media so as to tie together the identities coming from Twitter, Facebook, and so on, with the current information already gathered from previous relationships with the individuals, if possible.

SDA includes multiple configuration options for company profile, product categorization, aliases, and the data import method. The main use cases supported by SDA are brand management and lead generation. Because SDA can be tailored, it can also support generic use cases based on a company's need.

All the capabilities to extract values from unstructured text are provided by the AQL language (discussed earlier). The difference is additional extractors created specifically for the SDA accelerator. If you wanted to perform social data analytics with only InfoSphere Streams, you could use the prebuilt extractors already provided and augment them with your own to achieve similar capabilities of extracting buzz and sentiment.

NOTE   *Figure 4-4 does not show that IBM Watson Explorer can be added to an SDA implementation because it can access all the data in BigInsights and other repositories.*

Streams Development Environment

Before we get into the facilities provided by InfoSphere Streams for application development, we have to get back to the idea of operators because an operator is the high-level element used in an application.

As we discussed earlier, an operator can be thought of as being a thread of execution within an application. This is true for primitive operators, but an additional concept expands on it: composite operators.

Earlier, Figure 4-1 showed a simple Streams application that includes three operators. The application is composed of operators and itself can be considered a composite operator. A *composite operator* is a logical unit that is made up of multiple other operators. Because it is a logical unit, you can use it just like any other operator when putting together an application graph. The concept is recursive: a composite operator is made up of operators that can also be composite operators. Streams takes this one step further: an application graph is actually a composite operator.

The obvious benefits of composite operators are modularization and reuse. Because a composite operator is an operator, it can be used just like any other operator available in a project. There is only one implementation of the composite for potentially many instances of it in an application. A composite operator definition can also include parameters to change the behavior of a specific instance. Just like we saw earlier with the `FileSource` operator that uses parameters to identify the file location and other characteristics, the composite operator can do the same. These parameters can also be used to set the parameter values of the operators included in the composite. This makes reuse even more effective. This results in less code to maintain and only one copy of the code to modify when problems are found, the existing processing needs to be modified, or additional processing is required.

Note that we are talking about a logical construct that makes it easier for development and maintenance. When it comes to runtime, each primitive operator included in the composite operator runs separately, either on separate CPU cores or at least as separate threads of execution. The multiple copies of a composite operator are also different from each other at runtime. Figure 4-5 shows an example of a Streams graph using multiple composite operators.

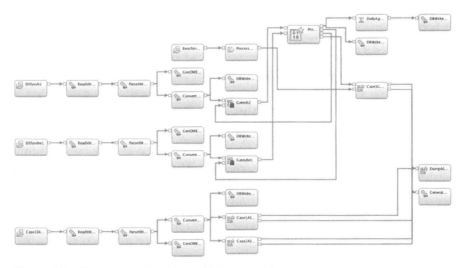

Figure 4-5   *Streams graph using multiple composite operators*

Figure 4-5 shows ReadXML, ParseXML, multiple DBWrite*, and others as composite operators, for a total of 18 composite operator instances coming from 10 composite operator definitions. The code itself was used in a successful proof-of-technology project. The other point this figure makes is that even this relatively small project ended up using over 30 operators in the application graph. We can see that it becomes easy to take advantage of the CPU cores available in a cluster. We also see that having proper development tools can greatly increase the productivity of the programming team, helping the programmer keep track of the relationship between the operators.

InfoSphere Streams comes with a compiler called sc that turns SPL into a runnable application. It can be used in makefiles and other methods of automating builds. Streams also comes with an integrated development environment called Streams Studio.

Streams Studio

Streams Studio is a set of Eclipse plug-ins, currently for Eclipse version 3.8.2. Eclipse is an integrated development environment that was originally developed by IBM Canada and released as open source in 2001. It is arguably the most popular Unix- or Linux-based development environment in the world.

Because Streams Studio is based on Eclipse, other plug-ins can be added to accommodate team development. For example, the svn plug-in for source control was tested and is working within Streams Studio. That way, source files can be shared, and developers can work on their own versions of different operators and share them once work on them is completed.

In addition to all the integrated development environment features included in Eclipse, Streams Studio comes with several specific productivity features:

- Task Launcher
- Text and visual editors
- Project Explorer
- Streams Explorer
- Cheat sheets
- Text analytics tooling

What follows is a brief description of these features.

Task Launcher

The Task Launcher includes a list of wizards divided into six tabs: Overview, Accelerate, Design, Develop, Publish and Run, and Visualize. The wizards include the following capabilities:

- Creating a Streams runtime instance
- Creating a Streams project

- Creating an SPL application
- Creating a Java primitive operator using a cheat sheet

Text and Visual Editors

The text editor includes features such as syntax highlighting and checking. The visual editor allows you to select operators and drop them into the canvas. It supports connecting operators to each other and editing their properties (such as port definitions and parameters).

Project Explorer

The Project Explorer is a view that helps keep track of all the components of a project. Other capabilities include importing new components, adding toolkit dependencies to the environment, and launching the application.

Streams Explorer

As the name implies, the Streams Explorer includes features to manage the runtime environment, such as starting and stopping instances, setting the log and trace levels, getting the logs, adding toolkit locations, and viewing the instance graph.

The instance graph is a visual representation of the running jobs, similar to the representation shown through the visual editor. It can color-code the operators in real time, showing their status visually. The capability is similar to that found in the Streams console, which we discuss in the "Streams Installation" and "Streams Administration" sections, later in the chapter.

Cheat Sheets

A cheat sheet is an interactive tool that guides you through the steps needed to accomplish a specific task. You saw earlier that cheat sheets are available through some wizards found in the Task Launcher. You can find all the cheat sheets under the Help menu. They include the following capabilities:

- Creating a C++ primitive operator
- Creating a C++ primitive operator with a shared library
- Creating a Java primitive operator
- Creating a native function

Text Analytics Tooling

The text analytics tooling is not installed in Streams Studio by default. Installing this tooling involves a few simple steps, but is a standard plug-in installation in Eclipse. The installation is needed only once per Streams Studio copy.

Text analytics is one of the most important subjects in big data analytics because a large quantity of new data arrives in the form of unstructured text. Having the proper tools makes a difference in the accuracy of the information extraction and the scalability of a solution.

Streams Studio shares the same text analytics tooling available in IBM InfoSphere BigInsights. Figure 4-6 shows the Streams Studio environment with an editor window open on an Annotation Query Language (AQL) source file. At the bottom of the figure is the Annotation Explorer showing the result of the execution of the AQL module, which also includes the name of the file processed, the context around the result (right and left), and which output view generated this result.

Figure 4-6 *Text analytics development environment*

Once the module is generating the appropriate results, you can easily use it in a Streams application by using the `TextExtract` operator and set the proper parameters to select the desired module. Adding the operator and setting its parameters can be done through the visual editor. Here is the actual code that would then be generated:

```
(stream<extractHighlight> TextExtract_H) as Extract1 =
TextExtract(Throttle_4_out0)
{
        param
                inputDoc   :  "data" ;
                moduleName:  "Mod1" ;
                modulePath:  "../textAnalytics/bin" ;
                tokenizer :  "multilingual" ;
                outputMode:  "multiPort" ;
}
```

The parameters identify the input tuple attribute that contains the text to process, the name of the module, its location, the tokenizer used to parse the document, and an output characteristic. At this point it is not important that you completely understand the code. This is simply an example that shows how easy it is to take advantage of the text analytics features within a Streams application.

The text analytics tooling includes the following features:

- Text editor
- Text analytics execution
- Best Practices Development Wizard
- Regular Expression Builder Wizard
- Regular Expression Generator Wizard
- Annotation Explorer

The tooling is continuously being improved. Likely, as this book becomes available, important features will be added to make the development of text analytics extractors easier.

Text analytics is one of the most important types of processing required in the age of big data. Real-time processing of unstructured text, especially when it comes to social media data, is critical to companies' competitiveness, and InfoSphere Streams provides the right features and tools to support a text analytics initiative.

Streams Installation

Because Streams is designed to run on clusters of machines, ease of installation is important because Streams may be required for hundreds of machines. The same is true when it comes time to upgrade to a newer, more feature-rich version.

Although it is possible to install Streams in a shared directory, it is better to install it on each machine separately to preserve network bandwidth. There is still a need for a shared directory for administrative purposes, but this is lightly used so it does not impact the network noticeably.

Streams installation focuses on making the process easy and less error prone. For example, the installation also verifies that the system meets the requirements for running the software. Streams provides four methods of installation:

- **Interactive GUI based** The installation is guided through a graphical interface.

- **Interactive console based** For systems that don't include a graphical interface, the interactive installation can be done through a standard Linux command-line console.

- **Interactive silent mode** The silent method uses a response file to guide the installation. This method is useful because it provides a repeatable process for installation on other nodes in the cluster. A sample response file is provided with the product as a starting point.

- **RPM-based installation** It is possible to create a customized RPM file that can then be used to install Streams on the nodes in the cluster.

The ability to easily install the product on a node in a cluster allows for faster cluster deployment. It is also easier to add nodes to a cluster as processing requirements increase.

Note that software upgrades are specific to the source and target versions of the product. The key here is that an upgrade path makes it easy to move to a newer version with minimal disruption to the production environment.

Streams Administration

Once an application goes into production, we need to ensure that the application runs efficiently and address any issues that may come up. InfoSphere Streams provides multiple tools and capabilities to provide a comprehensive view of the production environment. Streams supports two types of metrics: system metrics and user-defined metrics. Twenty-seven system metrics are defined that apply to input and output ports. The user-defined metrics are custom metrics that are part of an operator definition. Many of the operators that come with Streams include metrics.[3] It is also possible to create custom metrics in operators created in the course of a project.

The rest of this section briefly describes the tools available with InfoSphere Streams.

streamtool

Any management task you may want to execute can be done through the `streamtool` command-line utility. It is used as part of the installation and setup as well as for starting and stopping instances, starting and stopping jobs, and so on. Here is a simple example of the use of `streamtool` to list all the instances available:

```
$ streamtool lsinstance streams@streamsadmin
```

Having a command-line tool is essential for management. It allows for the automation of tasks through CRON jobs and the use of any other automatic monitoring techniques. This automation can greatly reduce the load on system managers, especially as the cluster gets larger.

A command-line utility may be perfect for automation, but for interactive monitoring, it is good to have GUI-based tools.

Instances Manager

The Instances Manager is a GUI-based utility that allows for the creation and removal of Streams instances. It also provides the ability to start and stop an instance. Figure 4-7 shows the Instances Manager screen.

Figure 4-7 *Instances Manager*

Streams Console

The Streams Console is a web-based tool that uses a secure connection (HTTPS). It can perform just about any task that can be done through the `streamtool` command, except for starting an instance (because the Streams Console requires a running instance). The Stream Console can be started either through the Instances Manager or by using the following `streamtool` command:

```
streamtool launch -i instance-id --console
```

Here, `instance-id` is the name of the instance to use.

The first screen to come up after starting the Streams Console is a login screen. Once the user is authenticated, a menu is displayed for the selection of the different management or monitoring tasks. Figure 4-8 shows an example of that screen.

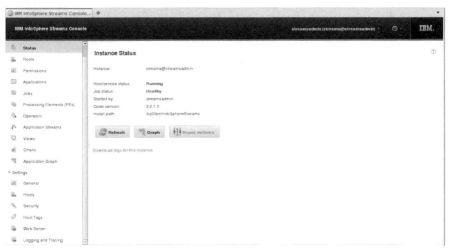

Figure 4-8 *Streams Console*

ReST API

In addition to the tools just described, InfoSphere Streams provides access to information on the health of the instances and jobs through a standard interface called Representational State Transfer (ReST). All the responses are returned in JSON format.

The ReST API provides a nice way to integrate Streams monitoring within existing tools. Note that this API extends to the ability to see data produced by application operators. This provides yet another integration capability—this time with applications having the proper permission.

Summary

This chapter explored the main components of InfoSphere Streams:

- Runtime
- Language
- Toolkits and accelerators

- Development tooling

- Installation and administration

We saw that the runtime is designed for scalability and performance and provides features such as security, scheduling, high availability, and recovery.

The Streams Processing Language (SPL) is designed with special features not found in standard programming languages because it has to support distributed processing of infinite streams of data and not just multithreading. The language also supports a recursive concept of operators that favors encapsulation and reuse.

InfoSphere Streams includes a large set of toolkits that provide useful operators, functions, and data types to support business processing. These capabilities provide tested processing elements that speed up development.

InfoSphere Streams includes a modern set of tools to support development and testing. The tools are based on the Eclipse platform, the most popular development platform on Unix-type systems. The tooling incorporates capabilities specific to the distributed real-time analytics development environment, including a visual editor, wizard, and cheat sheets. It also shares the same tooling as IBM BigInsights for text analytics development.

To conclude this chapter, we went through a brief overview of the installation, upgrade, and management capabilities, as well as discussed the comprehensive set of tools for production environments.

Endnotes

1. POWER8 systems have run the latest version of Streams, but it is not officially documented as supported at the time of this writing.

2. SDA currently only supports English and the North American locales.

3. http://www-01.ibm.com/support/knowledgecenter/SSCRJU_3.2.1/com.ibm.swg.im.infosphere.streams.dev.doc/doc/metricaccess.html?lang=en

5

The InfoSphere Streams Ecosystem

A distributed real-time analytics platform must integrate with the overall big data environment. It must fit seamlessly within the big data architecture and the enterprise legacy systems. This chapter describes how InfoSphere Streams interfaces with many of these systems. The following subjects are covered in this chapter:

- Adapters provided with Streams
- Open-source adapters
- IBM products interfaces
- Partner products interfaces
- Streams extensibility

The InfoSphere Streams ecosystem is constantly changing. Even though this chapter covers a wide range of products, this discussion should not be considered exhaustive.

Streams-Provided Adapters

As you saw in Chapter 4, InfoSphere Streams comes with a number of toolkits. Several toolkits include adapters used to communicate with the outside world. This section explores several of these toolkits.

Standard Toolkit Adapters

Operators from the standard toolkit are available by default to all projects. The standard toolkit provides the following adapters used to communicate with the outside world:

- **DirectoryScan, FileSource, and FileSink**   The names of these operators are enough to understand what they do. The FileSource adapter also has the ability to take its input from a source such as DirectoryScan that then provides the name of the next file to read. Each operator comes with a set of parameters that should give all the flexibility required in reading and writing files. The FileSource and DirectoryScan operators also come with custom output functions that provide yet more flexibility in implementations.

- **TCPSource and TCPSink**   These two operators provide input and output over a network connection of type TCP. The parameters provide the flexibility required to handle a variety of situations. Note that the TCPSource operator includes five assignment functions that allow for the retrieval of information about the remote host. It also has a function that returns the number of tuples processed.

- **UDPSource and UDPSink**   These two operators are similar to TCPSource and TCPSink but for the UDP protocol. Just like the other adapters mentioned, they use parameters to adjust to specific requirements, and the UDPSource adapter also includes several custom output functions.

- **XMLParse**   XML is a common information exchange format. The XMLParse operator is not strictly an adapter, but it is included here because it facilitates the transformation of XML communication by providing the means to convert XML documents into tuples. It includes the output functions XPath, XPathList, and XPathMap.

The adapters provided by the standard toolkit give the basic functionality for file and network I/O. Other toolkits, such as internet and messaging, provide higher-level protocol support, as you will see later.

Big Data Toolkit Adapters

This toolkit is used to interface with IBM BigInsights, IBM Big SQL, and IBM Watson Explorer. It should be noted that the Hadoop distributed file system (HDFS) operators can be used with other Hadoop distributions such as Cloudera.

BigInsights

BigInsights is IBM's Hadoop distribution. The current release is version 3.0. It includes the usual Hadoop-related products and also multiple added-value components, as depicted in Figure 5-1.

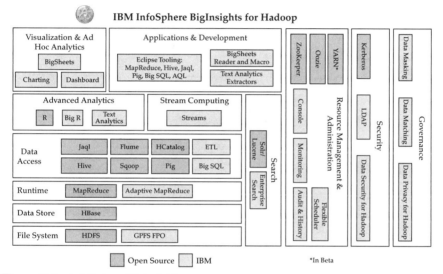

Figure 5-1 *InfoSphere BigInsights*

InfoSphere Streams interfaces with BigInsights in multiple ways. It has operators that are used to read and write to the Hadoop file system. BigInsights also supports an enhanced file system called GPFS-FPO (General Parallel File System File Placement Optimizer). Streams can also use this file system.

Another way that Streams integrates with BigInsights is through the social data analytics accelerator mentioned in Chapter 4. In addition, a set of toolkits interfaces with other Hadoop components, as you'll see later in this chapter.

Big SQL

For a while now there has been growing interest in having an SQL interface to the Hadoop data. Most of the current implementations only offer a subset of SQL syntax capabilities. BigInsights version 3.0 introduces a new SQL interface called Big SQL. Its architecture is shown in Figure 5-2.

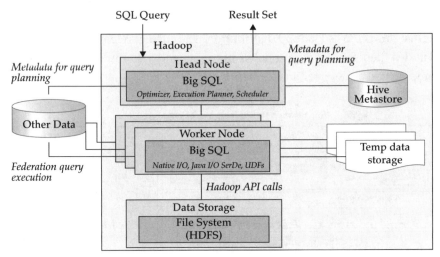

Figure 5-2   *Big SQL architecture*

The Big SQL processor supports a much more complete SQL language, to the point where it can run all of the 99 TPC-DS benchmark queries as well as the 22 TPC-H queries without modification. Note that performance was an important component of the overall design. Big SQL can also run federated queries with commercial relational database products such as Oracle, Teradata, and more.

InfoSphere Streams can interface with Big SQL as yet another relational repository, as you'll see in the upcoming database toolkit discussion.

Watson Explorer

Chapter 1 mentioned the need for a big data architecture. The IBM Big Data architecture is actually known as Watson Foundations. The Watson Explorer product is part of this architecture and is able to interact with both BigInsights and Streams.

Watson Explorer can consolidate and visualize information across enterprise applications and big data assets to help organizations discover, analyze, and integrate their data in a unified view. Figure 5-3 shows the overall Watson Explorer application architecture.

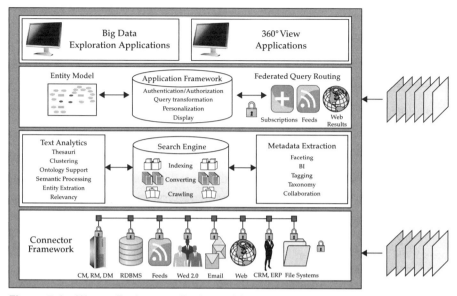

Figure 5-3 *Watson Explorer application architecture*

Watson Explorer also supports text analytics. This capability is based on the Annotation Query Language (AQL), which is a common component with BigInsights and Streams.

InfoSphere Streams can update Watson Explorer in real time, making Watson Explorer more responsive to real-time analytics needs. Because Watson Explorer visualizes data, it is also a way to visualize some of the data processed by Streams.

Database Toolkit Adapters

The database toolkit adapters provide access to the following specific database products:

- Aster
- HP Vertica
- IBM Big SQL
- IBM DB2
- IBM Informix

- IBM Netezza
- IBM SolidDB
- Microsoft SQL Server
- MySQL
- Oracle
- Teradata

The biggest issue over the support of database products is the availability of an ODBC driver for the desired product available on the target Linux and hardware platforms. The ODBC drivers are provided by the database vendors. Because these operators access databases through ODBC, it should also be possible to access databases not listed as supported as long as there are ODBC drivers for them.

The parameters included in the operators provide information on connection and reconnection policies. Many operators also support an optional control input port that gives the ability to change the database used, the username, and the password, as well as initiate a disconnect or reconnect operation. These capabilities make for a more dynamic solution and add to the flexibility of a solution.

Financial Services Toolkit Adapters

The adapters provided with the financial services toolkit are used to translate back and forth the external formats from different financial sources and targets. The following formats and protocols are supported:

- Financial Information eXchange (FIX)
- WebSphere Front Office for Financial Markets (WFO)
- WebSphere MQ Low-Latency Messaging (LLM)
- Simulated Market Feeds (Equity Trades and Quotes, Option Trades)

WFO is a market data delivery platform that provides feed handlers for over 100 data feeds, including major American, European, and Asian data sources. It also supports the creation of custom feed handlers. The toolkit includes two adapters: one to read from WFO and another to write to it.

LLM is designed for near instantaneous and reliable delivery of extremely large volumes of data. The toolkit provides one adapter to write to an LLM queue.

DataStage Integration Toolkit

IBM InfoSphere DataStage is a popular Extract, Transform, and Load (ETL) tool that is the core product module of the InfoSphere Information Server information integration platform. It is a key component of an overall big data architecture.

DataStage can integrate a variety of data sources through the use of modular processing, which can take advantage of multiple cores and parallel processing to provide needed scalability for increasing volumes of data. This is illustrated in Figure 5-4.

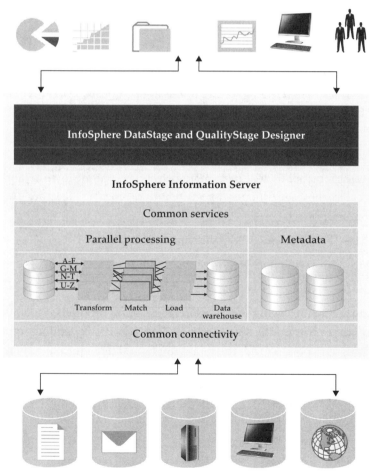

Figure 5-4   *InfoSphere DataStage high-level processing architecture*

DataStage includes a complete development environment and is optimal for data integration tasks.

InfoSphere Streams integrates with DataStage in two ways: it can get data from DataStage and it can send data to it. Streams can use DataStage to enrich its data, or it can take advantage of specialized processing already available in DataStage. DataStage can use Streams for such capabilities as text analytics and data mining using the analytics models developed through specialized tools such as SPSS.

Streams and DataStage can complement each other to provide a better integration within a big data architecture.

Internet Toolkit Adapter

The internet toolkit comes with one operator called Inet Source. This operator provides periodic retrieval of textual data from a list of uniform resource identifiers (URIs) over the following protocols: HTTP, HTTPS, FTP, and FTPS. It also supports retrieving RSS feeds data over HTTP and HTTPS.

Messaging Toolkit Adapters

The messaging toolkit includes three sets of operators to read and write messages to message queues for different protocols. Here are the three protocols supported:

- **XMS**   For WebSphere MQ versions 7.0, 7.1, and 7.5
- **JMS**   For WebSphere MQ version 7.5 and Apache ActiveMQ version 5.7
- **MQTT**   For MQTT version 3.1

Because it is interfacing with specific messaging products, Streams needs to have the appropriate software installed for it. Depending on which messaging transport is used, the following would be required:

- **XMS**   A WebSphere MQ server, WebSphere MQ client, and XMS client
- **JMS**   If WebSphere is used, it requires a WebSphere MQ server and a WebSphere MQ Java client
- **MQTT**   An MQTT client

MQTT is a relatively new protocol. It was invented back in 1999, and IBM submitted version 3.1 as a communication standard to the OASIS consortium. As of January 2014, the OASIS MQTT technical committee submitted a draft standard for review.

MQTT is important because it was designed as a machine-to-machine (M2M), Internet of Things (IoT) protocol and is supported by multiple companies, including IBM, Red Hat, Software AG, Inc., TIBCO Software, Inc., and VMware, Inc.[1] MQTT is technically important because it is designed to minimize network bandwidth usage and resource requirements. It is already used in multiple projects, and with the explosion of connected sensors everywhere, we can expect its popularity to increase.

Mining Toolkit

The mining toolkit executes business models for classification, clustering, regression, and associations over streaming data. It does not include any adapters to interface with the outside world, but it is included here because it supports the Predictive Model Markup Language (PMML), a standard language that can be generated from state-of-the-art statistics and data-mining software tools such as InfoSphere Warehouse, R/Rattle, SAS Enterprise Miner, SPSS, and Weka.

The implementation supports algorithms coming from InfoSphere Warehouse. For each algorithm, a specific range of PMML versions is supported. Consult the documentation for additional details.

SPSS also provides its own integration with InfoSphere Streams. This is covered later in the chapter.

R-Project Toolkit

The R language and environment has seen a surge in popularity in recent years. It is now integrated in multiple products, including IBM PureData Systems for Analytics (using Revolution R Enterprise) and several Hadoop distribution providers such as IBM BigInsights.

Some claim that R is popular because it is a package written by statisticians for statisticians. R includes quality algorithms covering subjects such as linear and nonlinear modeling and time series analysis. It also includes graphical capabilities. In fact, a large repository of packages is available in the Comprehensive R Archive Network (CRAN).[2] The packages are divided into 33 "tasks" covering subjects including the following:

- Econometrics
- Environmetrics
- Machine learning
- Medical imaging
- Natural language processing
- Pharmacokinetics
- Spatiotemporal
- Time series

This partial list should give you an idea of the breadth of the subjects covered.

The InfoSphere Streams R-project toolkit `RScript` operator not only allows you to execute an R program on incoming tuples, but also includes an optional input port that accepts a string representing the path to an R program. It is used to update or replace the analytic code in the initialization or processing scripts. Add to that the parallel execution capabilities of InfoSphere Streams, and a programmer has all the flexibility needed to implement a solution that takes full advantage of the available processing algorithm capabilities of R.

ReST API

The discussion of the Streams capabilities for interfacing with the outside world would not be complete without a mention of the ReST API. As stated in Chapter 4, Streams supports the ReST API for accessing all manner of attributes of the running system. It includes administrative information as well as the ability to make data coming from the output ports of given operators available. This means that the ReST API provides a way to integrate InfoSphere Streams with any extensible product that supports the ReST API. This includes system management programs as well as dashboard-like products.

Open-Source Toolkits

InfoSphere Streams comes with a large set of integration capabilities, as discussed in the previous sections. Also, a community of developers contribute additional toolkits available in the form of source code (open source).

The open-source toolkits are not directly supported by IBM, but instead by the open-source community. There is also synergy between the Streams product and the toolkits put out as open source. In the past, some toolkits on a community site were eventually pulled into the product and became fully supported toolkits. This practice should continue in the future.

There are currently two main locations where these open-source toolkits are available:

- **Streams Exchange**   The Streams Exchange is a community for developers to share information. Most often, the content that is shared will consist of source code and associated information about the source code.

  Streams Exchange includes three contribution sections: Streams toolkits, Streams applications, and Streams tools.

- **GitHub**   GitHub is a collaborative site for open-source and private projects. A number of Streams-related open-source projects can be found on this site. Several projects are grouped under the IBMStreams directory, but there are other projects on their own. These projects are likely to eventually be moved under IBMStreams.

Consult this book's appendix for the URLs for these sites. The Streams exchange was the original repository for open source. However, an effort is underway to move the Streams Exchange code to GitHub. In the meantime, we have to visit two separate sites.

Both Streams Exchange and GitHub include toolkits that can be used for integration. On Streams exchanges, the following two toolkits can be considered to fit this description:

- **OpenCV toolkit**   The OpenCV toolkit takes its name from the OpenCV open-source library of the same name. This toolkit also has dependencies on the ffmpeg library. The OpenCV toolkit operators provide capabilities for ingesting images from files, cameras, or web servers and analyzing them with "open source computer vision" algorithms.

- **Accumulo toolkit**   The Accumulo toolkit integrates Streams with another part of the Hadoop big data offering. It provides access to Apache Accumulo by exposing its API to Streams. As expected, it requires the Accumulo, Zookeeper, and Hadoop libraries to work properly.

On the GitHub site, the following toolkits (under IBMStreams) can be useful for integration:

- **streamsx.hbase**   This toolkit is another integration point with the Hadoop ecosystem. It allows for reading and writing to Apache HBase. It has been tested with HBase 0.94.3 and Hadoop 1.1.0, but is expected to work for any later version of Hadoop or HBASE.

- **streamsx.inet**   The inet toolkit supports common Internet protocols as well as the following functionality:

  - General-purpose Internet operators supporting a number of protocols

  - Operators that interact with external HTTP servers

  - Operators that embed an HTTP server to provide a ReST-style API for streaming data

  - Operators that embed a WebSocket server to expose streaming data as WebSocket messages

- **Resource Managers**   This subdirectory currently includes an implementation for only one resource manager: YARN (Yet Another Resource Negotiator). It provides an integration point with Hadoop environments because YARN is becoming the Hadoop resource manager of choice. This way, Streams can run in the Hadoop environment and its resources accounted for in the global context of the Hadoop cluster.

- **streamsx.json**   The json toolkit does not provide a new way to communicate with the outside world, but can still be considered an integration toolkit because it provides an easy-to-use interface for processing JSON documents to generate tuples and to generate JSON documents from Streams tuples.

- **streamsx.messaging**   This project includes a release subdirectory that contains the following operators:

  - The `MQTTSource` and `MQTTSink` operators are implemented in Java and work with the Eclipse Paho Java client.

  - The `KafkaProducer` and `KafkaConsumer` operators are for subscribing and publishing data to Kafka servers.

  The MQTT operators are actually improved implementations of the operators currently provided with Streams. Kafka is a popular open-source messaging system. The Kafka operators provide the appropriate integration with it.

The open-source community is quite active. The contents of these repositories (Streams Exchange and GitHub) are constantly changing, with regular new additions and improvements to the already provided toolkits. These sites should be visited regularly to see the new additions.

IBM Products' Interfaces

At this point we've already covered BigInsights, Big SQL, Watson Explorer, DataStage, WebSphere Front Office for Financial Markets (WFO), and WebSphere MQ Low-Latency Messaging (LLM). The integration is provided through the Streams toolkits. Some other important products also integrate with Streams. Note that the products covered here do not constitute an exhaustive list. Rather, this discussion shows how other products could also integrate with Streams.

SPSS

SPSS software is used to develop and deploy predictive analytic assets. These assets are developed using data-mining methodologies, where historical data is used to build predictive models. The SPSS team has developed a toolkit to provide the integration of Streams and SPSS. Figure 5-5 illustrates this integration through an example.

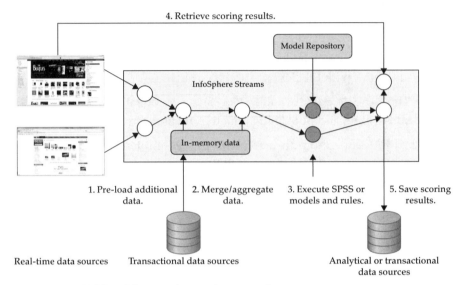

Figure 5-5   *SPSS and Streams integration example*

The figure shows the reading of multiple sources where Streams does some merging of information. Once the data is preprocessed, it can pass on the tuples to the SPSS scoring operator. The final step saves the scoring in a repository, and Streams can also do additional processing based on the scoring.

The general lifecycle of a predictive model application follows three main phases: development, deployment, and maintenance. For the integration with Streams, the development is done using SPSS Modeler. The deployment is done through the toolkit scoring operator. A model requires maintenance and updates based on new information. SPSS Collaboration and Deployment services provides the model management. Once a model is modified, it can be updated in a running Streams application. A lot of the big data challenge is about being able to derive actionable information from all the data available. SPSS is a state-of-the-art tool for the development and running of models to achieve this goal. The integration of SPSS with Streams extends this capability to real-time environments. Being able to determine the next best action in real time demonstrates the value of real-time analytics, the power of now.

IBM Operational Decision Manager (ODM)

InfoSphere Streams includes the Rules toolkit, used to integrate with IBM Operational Decision Manager (ODM). ODM is a platform for capturing, automating, and governing frequent, repeatable business decisions. It consists of two components used for managing and executing business rules and business events:

- **IBM Decision Center**   Provides integrated repository and management components, allowing subject matter experts to maintain and govern their business decisions.

- **IBM Decision Server**   Provides the runtime components to automate decision logic, enabling the detection of business situations and precise response based on the context of the interaction.

ODM is a business tool where business people can define a workflow for the development, verification, testing, and release of business rules. ODM integration with Streams is shown in Figure 5-6.

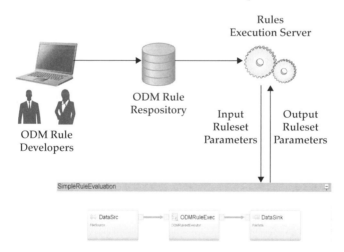

Figure 5-6   *ODM integration*

ODM rules are deployed to a repository. The `ODMRulesetExecutor` Streams operator has a parameter that identifies the repository and gets notifications when new rules or updated rules are deployed. The Streams application converts tuples to ruleset parameters and passes them to the

ODM Rule Execution Server. When the Streams application gets the results back, it converts them from ruleset parameters to tuples.

For the operator to be notified when rules are updated, it has to be set up with a TCP/IP connection to the ODM Management Console. This way, there is no need to interrupt the execution when new rules are put in place.

MessageSight

IBM MessageSight is a messaging appliance designed for machine-to-machine (M2M) and mobile environments. It processes large volumes of events in near real time and is ideal for Internet of Things (IoT) solutions. IBM MessageSight is capable of supporting 1 million concurrent sensors or smart devices and can scale up to 13 million messages per second.[3]

Because MessageSight uses the MQTT protocol, it is easily integrated within a Streams application using the messaging toolkit.

Partners and Third-Party Products

The wide range of adapters available with InfoSphere Streams makes it easy to integrate it with many environments. In this section we highlight some additional products that can integrate with Streams. You can find a list and description of Big Data partners, and specifically InfoSphere Streams partners, on the Business Partner Profiles page.[4] Listed are 28 partners that provide products and services. These partners work in areas such as the following:

- Consulting
- Geospatial services
- Social data provider
- Speech to text
- Solutions powered by Streams

Some of these partners specialize in specific industries, such as

- Government (including defense)
- Telecommunication
- Media and entertainment
- Healthcare/life sciences

Working with partners provides an additional source of solutions and experts to lead a Streams project to its successful conclusion.

Streams Extensibility

InfoSphere Streams is a platform for real-time distributed analytics. The provided capabilities are already substantial, but Streams has to be able to adjust to the changing business needs and the new technologies that answer those needs. Therefore, Streams includes ways to add new operators and functions through simple APIs. The Streams Studio IDE also has wizards to guide a developer in these tasks.

Developers have three approaches to adding functions and operators in the Streams environment: SPL, C++, and Java.

An SPL application is in fact a composite operator that is made up of other composite and primitive operators. Because the SPL language is a complete programming language that compiles to binary code, there are no performance penalties for using it. It is possible to write functions in SPL to use in operators. Streams has an operator called Custom that is a framework for an operator that allows programmers to include any processing of their choice. As long as the new functionality does not require the use of external libraries, using SPL to extend Streams capabilities is a perfectly good approach.

Streams supports the C++ language as a way to add operators and functions. With C++, it is possible to add the use of external libraries, as demonstrated by the OpenCV toolkit mentioned earlier. The C++ operators provide the most flexible way to write operators, including handling different stream types.

The third approach is to use Java, which is the language of choice when there is a need to integrate with existing Java libraries. For example, many open-source products are written in Java. It is then easy to use these products in a Streams application through new Java operators. Java operators are easy to write because the interface with Streams is defined through a simple operator API and the use of Java annotations. The Streams Studio IDE also includes a wizard that guides the developer through the steps of implementing an operator.

Streams extensibility is an essential feature that ensures that this environment can adjust to varied business needs as well as to future technological changes.

Summary

This chapter covered the numerous ways InfoSphere Streams can integrate in a business environment. The product itself comes with a set of toolkits that provide interfaces with many systems through files, network access, messaging, and so on.

The integration story continues with a community of people who support and enhance repositories of open-source toolkits to interface with such big data products as HBase and Accumulo. Streams can also process data in known formats such as JSON, and it also includes capabilities for images and video processing. The repositories are active and continue to expand as new capabilities become popular.

InfoSphere Streams also integrates with other popular IBM products such as SPSS and ODM, not to mention the database interfaces that then allow communications with IBM database products such as DB2, Informix, and Pure Data System for Analytics.

The Streams ecosystem would not be complete without a community of partners that provide products and expertise in many industries.

Even with all the capabilities provided for integration, InfoSphere Streams ensures that it can adjust to changing business needs by providing APIs and wizards so that anyone can add new functionality and integration points.

A data-in-motion product must have a solid ecosystem to ensure that it integrates with the existing business environments as well as the new systems introduced in development projects. A solid and extensive ecosystem also future-proofs a solution because it supports many integration methods and processing capabilities, as well as partners' solutions and expertise. InfoSphere Streams has what it takes for distributed real-time analytics applied to business problems in the demanding world of big data.

Endnotes

1. https://www.oasis-open.org/committees/tc_home.php?wg_abbrev=mqtt

2. http://cran.us.r-project.org/

3. http://www-03.ibm.com/press/us/en/pressrelease/40926.wss

4. http://www-01.ibm.com/software/data/bigdata/business-partners-profiles-isv.html

6
Getting Started

We've covered a lot of material in this book. In this chapter we look at how to get started with InfoSphere Streams and start putting together distributed real-time analytics solutions.

A lot of excellent material is available on the Web. The key is to use it in a way that allows for an orderly progression from neophyte to expert. The best way to start is to get your hands on the product and start coding. Once you get your first taste of the product, we can move on to more in-depth subjects.

This chapter covers the following subjects:

- How to get Streams
- Introductory hands-on lab
- Moving on to more in-depth learning
- Streamsdev and the Streams Playbook
- Navigating the documentation
- Other available material location

You can find the URL references for the material needed in your learning journey in this book's appendix.

How to Get Streams

InfoSphere Streams can be hosted on the cloud, in a virtual machine, or on dedicated hardware. At the time of this writing, the latest available version is 3.2.1.1 (version 3.2.1, fix pack 1). It comes in multiple editions:

- IBM InfoSphere Streams (Production)
- IBM InfoSphere Streams Developer Edition
- IBM InfoSphere Streams for Non-Production Environment
- IBM InfoSphere Streams Quick Start Edition

The Quick Start Edition is available as a free download from the IBM website.[1] This edition does not include the accelerators mentioned in Chapter 4. However, this is not a problem because we are talking about learning the product and not developing production applications.

The Quick Start Edition is available as a software download or as an already installed product in a VMware image. Using the VMware image is the quickest way to start learning Streams. It includes the introductory lab covered in the next section.

The VMware image is a 4GB download. Note that the image runs a 64-bit guest operating system, so the host system must support that. The image is set to use 2GB of memory (RAM) and two CPUs. The host operating system should have 4GB of memory or more and a four-core CPU. Running the image requires VMware Workstation 8.x or newer or a current version of VMware Player (free for Windows or Linux) or VMware Fusion (Mac).

Introductory Hands-on Lab

The introductory lab is designed to get the user developing an application using the visual editor of Streams Studio. It is part of the Quick Start Edition VMware image, so there is nothing more to install. The instructions for the lab are found on the Streamsdev site, which we cover in detail later in this chapter.

The lab is divided into four parts, starting with a blank slate and eventually leading to the application shown in Figure 6-1.

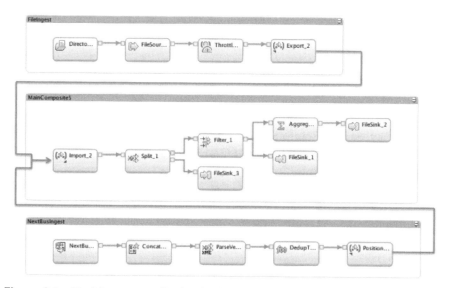

Figure 6-1 *Final Streams application for the introductory lab*

The application demonstrates the modularization of a Streams application into three parts. The top block, `FileIngest`, shows data ingestion from files read from a directory. The bottom block, `NextBusIngest`, shows ingesting data from a live Internet feed. The middle block, `MainComposite5`, is the main application that processes the data. Each block is independent from each other. `FileIngest` and `NextBusIngest` export their data to a named entity, and `MainComposite5` reads from that named entity. This way, a new ingestion method can be added and old ones removed without interrupting the processing.

As mentioned earlier, the lab is divided into four parts. It starts with a simple application so as to familiarize the student with the environment, creating a project, and putting together a few operators. Each subsequent part adds to the previous one and introduces new concepts such as monitoring a running application and using simple visualization of the data processed.

Because each part builds on the previous one, the lab comes with five workspaces. The first four represent the starting points for their respective parts, and the fifth workspace is the completed application. This way, the student can move forward even if something went wrong in the current part. Keep in mind that making mistakes is the best way to learn.

Moving on to More In-depth Learning

After doing the introductory lab, you are ready to move to more in-depth learning. Before diving into SPL, it is a good idea to get an overview of the components of a Streams application and of the language. Several videos can be found on YouTube that help with this. A good starting point is the Developer Education series, which includes the following videos:

- Intro to Streams Computing
- Building Blocks
- Components
- Application Design and Jobs
- Runtime
- Advanced Concepts
- The SPL Language

The SPL language is relatively easy to learn. It includes a declarative part that allows for the definition of the operators and their relationships. You partially learned this through the introductory lab by working in the graphical editor that basically defines these declarations. This has the secondary benefit that you do not have to remember the exact syntax for hand-coding because it is so easy to generate this and then see the exact syntax in the text editor and work from there if needed.

There are a few keys to becoming fluent in the declarative part of SPL. The first one is to understand the concepts of ports and streams. An operator may have multiple ports as input as well as output. An input port can receive multiple streams of data as long as they have the same tuple definition. This is illustrated in Figure 6-2.

In this figure, we see the three operators on the left, each with one output port generating an output stream. The Process operator has two ports.

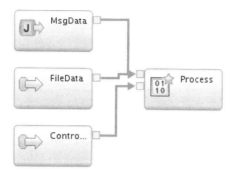

Figure 6-2   *Ports and streams*

The first one receives two streams—one from `MsgData` and one from `FileData`. The second port receives one stream. Sometimes when you're reading through the documentation, the difference may seem unclear. Hopefully, this short explanation is all you'll need to understand the difference.

The second key to fluency in SPL is to know the operators available. SPL comes with multiple toolkits that include close to 100 operators. They are well divided functionally, so it is simply a matter of remembering that there is an operator for a given purpose and going to the documentation to get the details, including the exact name. Streams Studio also helps because it provides a quick way to search for operators and also includes a parameter selection dialog for each operator edited. We cover navigating the documentation later in this chapter.

The second part of SPL is the procedural language. Experienced programmers should find the language very familiar because it is so similar to C. The main new concepts to get used to are that variables must be explicitly declared as "mutable" if they are not used as constants and that casting can only be done explicitly.[2] Because any coding errors related to these features are caught at compile time, any problems can be resolved early.

The SPL Lab

The SPL lab instructions can also be found on the Streamsdev site. Figure 6-3 provides an overview of the SPL artifacts being developed through the lab.

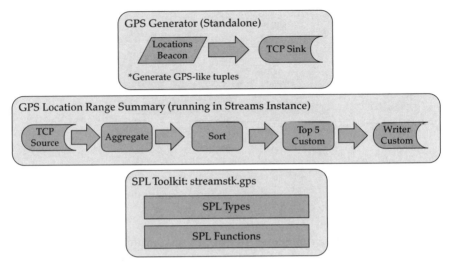

Figure 6-3 *SPL lab overview*

Even though we want to focus on the SPL procedural language part, it is impossible to do a Streams lab without operators. The procedural code is there to complement the declaration of operators. This is why the lab uses a set of operators but also has a section with SPL types and SPL functions.

The lab is divided into four parts. The first part starts with a simple "Hello World!" type application. The second part dives into creating types and functions. It leads to the third and fourth parts, where the procedural code is used in conjunction with multiple operators.

Other Labs

The content of Streamsdev is constantly changing. At the time of this writing, the following additional labs were available:

- **R Toolkit lab** This lab shows how to use the R statistical language in Streams using the RScript operator. It requires the installation of the open-source product R.[3]

- **Rules (ODM) lab** This lab shows the integration of Streams with IBM Operational Decision Manager. ODM must be installed to run this lab.

Additional Topics

Several additional topics should be looked at to round out one's Streams knowledge. They include the following:

- Learning the operators
- Understanding how to use composite operators
- Java and C++ primitive operators development

These subjects are presented in a logical order that helps with the learning progression.

Learning the Operators

All the operators in InfoSphere Streams are useful. The best approach is to spend some time reading through the operators in the standard toolkit and go over the ones in the specialized toolkits as needed.

The operators `Aggregate`, `Join`, `Sort`, and `Custom` are of particular interest—the first three because they use the windowing concept to work on a set of tuples, and the last one because it is a blank slate to implement just about anything you want.

The `Custom` operator is the first level for creating a user-defined operator. It is very powerful, and because the SPL language is complete, just about any processing can be done through it as long as you don't need the assistance of an external library. The drawback is that it is an addictive operator: it is easy to take the view that everything requires a custom operator. Be warned that you need to make sure you understand the value of all the operators provided with Streams.

Understanding How to Use Composite Operators

A composite operator is a great way to modularize a project. Even a composite operator containing only one operator is a useful construct because it can include the setting of multiple parameters as default values, and you can reuse it instead of having to set the parameters multiple times in multiple areas of a project.

The key capability to learn is how to use parameters in a composite operator. This is powerful since it provides a means to pass values to the operators included in the composite and set their parameters. Composite operator parameters even let you pass in type, function, and operator name.

Java and C++ Primitive Operators Development

Creating a primitive operator can be considered the ultimate expertise level. Not every project needs this, so there is no reason to rush into it. In some cases, the Custom operator is all that is needed to customize the environment.

InfoSphere Streams actually makes it easy to create primitive operators in Java through the use of annotations and guidance through a cheat sheet. Writing a Java operator would be the easiest path for native operators.

The choice of language can also depend on which libraries are required in a specific project. If the library is in Java, Java becomes the logical choice. For ultimate performance, primitive operators should be written in C++. This development is made easier because Streams Studio also includes cheat sheets for the development of C++ primitive operators.

Streams Studio and Other Tools

Up to now, the focus of our discussion has been on learning the language and the constructs around it. We need to also pay attention to the tools available for development and monitoring. Note that videos are available to introduce some of these tools and make it easier to get up to speed. They can be found on the Streamsdev site, which we discuss next.

Streamsdev and the InfoSphere Streams Playbook

Two sites aim at providing a centralized repository of information about Streams. They are the InfoSphere Streams Playbook and Streamsdev. The Playbook was designed as a source of information for people new to Streams. The site includes the following main sections:

- **Reference material**   This is where we will find all the links related to the Information Center and the available redbooks, for example.

- **Video tutorials**   This section points you to a set of videos that will help you get up to speed with InfoSphere Streams.

- **Video use cases**   In here, you will find uses cases in video or text format. This will help you understand how InfoSphere Streams can be applied to multiple industries and business problems.

- **Other use cases**   This section describes additional use cases, but not in video format.

- **Ecosystem**   This section provides information on the use of InfoSphere Streams with other software products, from IBM or otherwise. This is not an exhaustive list of products that can interact with InfoSphere Streams, but rather a glimpse at the possibilities.

- **Developer corner**   This section provides links to development resources and examples of Streams programming.

- **Streams on GitHub**   This section provides a short description of the Streams projects available on GitHub.

The Streamsdev site's original intent was to provide information for developers, by developers. It was created for a different audience. Since its inception, however, its goals have evolved to include information relevant to people new to Streams. For this reason, the content of the Playbook is being migrated to Streamsdev. Because the migration is still in progress, both sites are still useful. Eventually, the Playbook should become a subset of Streamsdev. If or when this happens, it will be noted in the Playbook so as to redirect people to Streamsdev. Eventually, the Playbook will be removed.

Streamsdev Details

Figure 6-4 shows a portion of the main Streamsdev landing page.

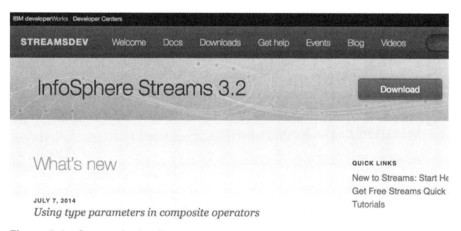

Figure 6-4   *Streamsdev landing page*

The second bar from the the top contains links that lead to other pages. The links are as follows:

- **STREAMSDEV** This is a link back to the landing page, wherever you are on the site.

- **Welcome** This includes pages similar to the Playbook, with descriptions of the site content, ecosystem, and so on.

- **Docs** The Docs section groups information in sections, including labs, articles, and how-to videos.

- **Downloads** A simple page with links to the Quick Start Edition download, its README file, and a pointer to the infocenter documentation. The name "infocenter" was used in an earlier implementation of the online documentation. Despite the name used, it really directs the user to the newer implementation called the knowledge center.

- **Get help** This section contains links to multiple useful sites, including the support portal and the Streams forum. It also has a way to submit requests for enhancements.

- **Events** This is an event calendar that shows public events such as meet-ups and virtual conferences. The calendar shows the current month.

- **Blogs** This page contains blog entry summaries from the newest to the oldest. It spans quite a few pages at this point. The topics are usually technical on how to accomplish specific tasks. Note that each entry title is a link to the complete blog entry.

- **Videos** At the time of this writing, this section contains links to 65 videos related to Streams. The menu on the left provides a way to see videos in specific categories and makes it easier to navigate. The videos can also be sorted by date, views, and likes.

The last thing in the second bar from the top of every page is a search. As expected, this is a way to search the site based on search strings.

There is one more thing to note about navigating Streamsdev. Figure 6-5 shows a portion of the Docs page that helps explain the navigation.

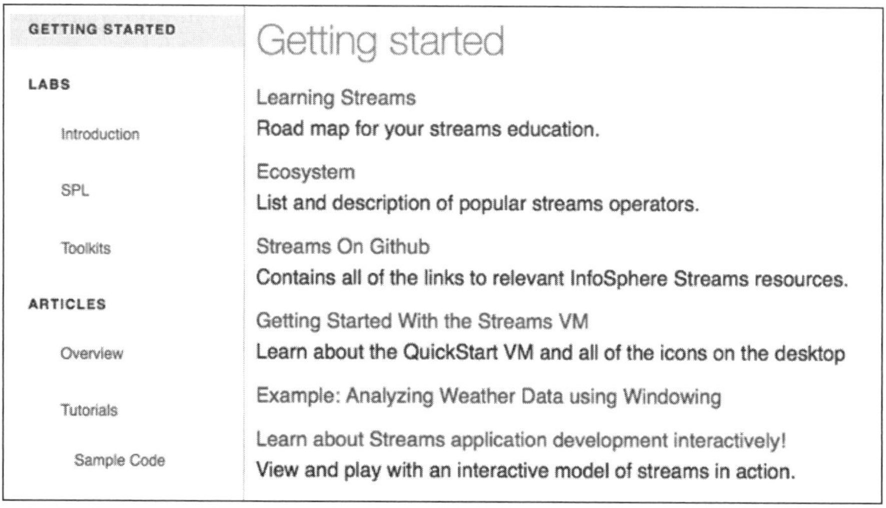
GETTING STARTED
LABS
Introduction
SPL
Toolkits
ARTICLES
Overview
Tutorials
Sample Code
Getting started
Learning Streams
Road map for your streams education.
Ecosystem
List and description of popular streams operators.
Streams On Github
Contains all of the links to relevant InfoSphere Streams resources.
Getting Started With the Streams VM
Learn about the QuickStart VM and all of the icons on the desktop
Example: Analyzing Weather Data using Windowing
Learn about Streams application development interactively!
View and play with an interactive model of streams in action.

Figure 6-5 *Portion of the Streamsdev Docs page*

All the lines in the menu on the left are active links. This includes Getting Started, Labs, and Articles in this figure. It is the same on the Videos page, with the additional subtlety that the little triangle (sometimes called a twisty) preceding the item indicates that it can be opened and includes additional subdivisions. Figure 6-6 shows the Video menu with an open item.

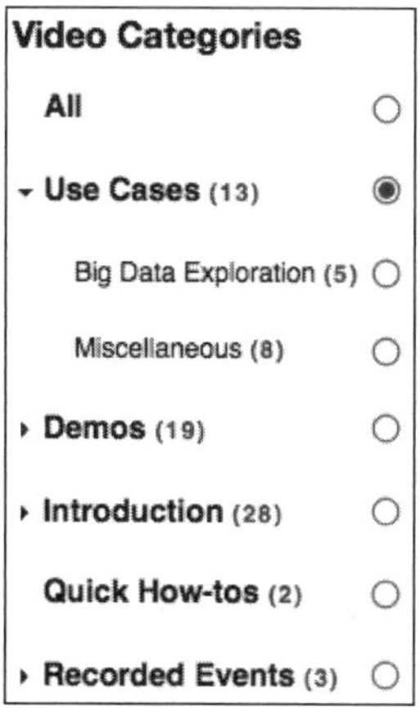
Video Categories
All
Use Cases (13)
Big Data Exploration (5)
Miscellaneous (8)
Demos (19)
Introduction (28)
Quick How-tos (2)
Recorded Events (3)

Figure 6-6 *Video page menu*

As you get more knowledgeable about Streams, you will find more and more interesting material on the Streamsdev site. Because blog entries are added at least weekly, it is a good idea to check the site at least once a week.

Navigating the Streams Documentation

The InfoSphere Streams documentation is available online. It can be found in a website repository called the knowledge center. The main Streams documentation page provides links to the documentation for all the available versions. This way, a developer can always get to the version in use in her project, but also can stay informed by looking at the latest documentation.

The knowledge center provides the ability to select a section of the documentation and generate a PDF version of it. This is a useful feature, especially when a developer works extensively in one area and constantly refers to the documentation for details. This way, she can have quicker access without depending on a network connection.

It is a good idea to spend some time going over the documentation cover to cover at least once. In the course of a project, some sections are referenced more than others. We cover this next. The documentation includes the following sections:

- **Welcome** The Welcome section includes a table of pointers to several subjects of interest and other information.

- **Product overview** This section includes a documentation roadmap, information on the new features and changes included in this specific release of the product, and the release notes. It also has an introduction to InfoSphere Streams and the accelerators.

- **Installing** This section covers the installation and upgrade of InfoSphere Streams as well as the installation of the IBM Accelerator for Social Data Analytics and the IBM Accelerator for Telecommunications Event Data Analytics.

- **Configuring** This section covers the Streams post-installation steps.

- **Tutorials** The Tutorials section includes three simple tutorials on writing a Streams application.

- **Administering** As expected, this section covers the creation and administration of Streams instances, including security, monitoring, and more.

- **Accelerating big data analytics** This section covers the use of the social data and telecommunication analytics accelerators. Note that you should also reference the BigInsights documentation on the social data analytics accelerator.

- **Developing** The Developing section includes a lot of information on varied and related subjects such as best practices, using Streams Studio, developing primitive operators, debugging, and more.

- **Troubleshooting** This section provides information on how to isolate and resolve problems.

- **Reference** Once familiar with InfoSphere Streams, a programmer will spend most of her time in this section. It includes information on the language, toolkits, and commands, among other things.

- **Glossary** The glossary is an alphabetized definition of terms.

This list gives us an idea of where to go to get information when performing a specific task. Certain subjects are constantly being referenced. Here is a list of some of the most referenced and their locations:

- **Expression operators** These are the parts of the SPL language such as the symbols for addition and subtraction. A table listing all the operators can be found under Reference -> Streams processing language reference -> Expression language -> Expression operators.

- **Built-in functions** This includes functions to manipulate collections, files, strings, and so on. They are located under Reference -> Toolkits -> SPL standard toolkit -> Builtin SPL Functions.

- **Types** This includes types, suffixes, and string escape characters. These are located in Reference -> Streams processing language reference -> Types.

- **Operator invocation** We can add operators to an application using the Streams Studio graphical editors. In some cases, it is useful to modify the invocation definition using the text editor. For this reason, we need to be familiar with the structure of an operator invocation. An operator invocation includes multiple clauses. They are described under Reference -> Streams processing language reference -> Operators -> Operator invocations.

This short list of essential documentation references will help any programmer new to Streams find the answers needed and quickly become productive in Streams projects. Of course, a lot more great information can be found in the documentation, and the search capability is another tool in the knowledge center that can help locate specific subjects.

Text Analytics

Text analytics is a very important subject in the big data world, especially when considering the processing of social media data. InfoSphere Streams includes a specialized toolkit called the Text toolkit. It contains one operator, `TextExtract`, that is used to execute extractors written in a language called AQL.

The Streams documentation includes a good deal of information on the AQL language under the Text toolkit. Still, some important details are left out, such as the details of the languages supported and the prebuilt extractors available. This is due to the fact that the AQL tooling comes from the BigInsights product. If you are interested in text analytics, you should also consult the BigInsights documentation, where you'll find the following interesting headings:

- Analyzing big data -> Analyzing big data with Text Analytics -> Text Analytics framework -> Multilingual support for Text Analytics

- Analyzing big data -> Analyzing big data with Text Analytics -> Developing Text Analytics extractors -> Pre-built extractor libraries

- Reference -> Text Analytics reference

The BigInsights documentation is also part of the knowledge center. The URL can be found in this book's appendix.

Other Material

There is nothing like having sample code to speed up learning and development, and there are several sources of sample code, either straight as examples or as supplemental to articles. This section gives some pointers on where to find sample code.

The Nifty Fifty

This set of examples started as 50 examples of the use of Streams operators. Since its beginning, the list has grown to around 80 examples. Here is a sample of the subjects covered as a list of directory names:

- 001_hello_world_in_spl
- 007_split_at_work
- 014_sort_at_work
- 015_join_at_work
- 016_aggregate_at_work
- 025_dynamic_filter_at_work
- 059_dynamic_scaleout_of_streams_application

This short list shows simple examples using different operators, but the list has grown to include more complex topics such as dynamic processing. The "nifty fifty" can be found in the InfoSphere Streams Quick Start Edition in the streamsadmin home directory under SPL-Examples-For-Beginners. These examples and a short description document can also be found on the Streams Exchange site under "Streams Applications (SPL)."

The Streams GitHub directory also includes a samples subdirectory that includes some sample code. At the time of this writing, the list included the following:

- DSPFilterBandpassExample
- DbLoader
- HDFSFormatter
- WindowTest

There is also a good chance that the Streams Exchange content will get migrated to GitHub and provide one location for all examples. Note that because all the Streams GitHub code comes with source, it can be seen as yet another source of sample code.

DeveloperWorks

The IBM DeveloperWorks website has been hosting technical information for years. In fact, InfoSphere Streams Playbook, Streamsdev, and Streams Exchange are all hosted by it.

You can find technical articles of interest at this site. Here are a few of the titles available:

- "Integrate InfoSphere Streams with InfoSphere Data Explorer"[4]
- "Using InfoSphere Streams with memcached and Redis"
- "InfoSphere Streams text analytics"
- "Get to know the R-project Toolkit in InfoSphere Streams"
- "Using InfoSphere Streams with Informix"

Note that the articles often come with a download link for the code presented in the article.

Documentation Sample Code

The InfoSphere Streams documentation includes several tutorials. The Tutorial section includes three tutorials and one example (VWAP). The Developing section includes a tutorial section with two tutorials.

Summary

This chapter gives a roadmap to learning InfoSphere Streams and a list of the most important sources of information on the product. The first step is to get your hands on the product to develop practical expertise. To help in this area, a few labs are available to help you quickly get familiar with the product. The rest of the chapter listed useful resources on learning Streams, including labs, tutorials, sample code, and articles.

By following this roadmap, a programmer can quickly become fluent with InfoSphere Streams and, over time, become an expert.

Endnotes

1. http://www-01.ibm.com/software/data/infosphere/streams/quick-start/
2. Except in declarations; see the documentation for details.
3. http://www.r-project.org/
4. InfoSphere Data Explorer is now Watson Explorer.

Appendix
Resources and References

This appendix lists the material mentioned in this book. Descriptions are included to provide some context.

Documentation

Two sites were mentioned in this book. Note that they point to the welcome page, which includes a selection for the version of the documentation desired:

- **InfoSphere BigInsights knowledge center**
  http://www-01.ibm.com/support/knowledgecenter/SSPT3X/SSPT3X_welcome.html

- **InfoSphere Streams knowledge center**
  http://www.ibm.com/support/knowledgecenter/SSCRJU/SSCRJU_welcome.html

Wikis

Although a few wiki sites were mentioned in this book, Streamsdev is likely the first site you should access in this list.

- **InfoSphere Streams Playbook (can also be found through a Google search)**
  https://www.ibm.com/developerworks/community/wikis/home?lang=en#!/wiki/InfoSphere%20Streams%20Playbook

- **Streamsdev**
  https://ibm.co/streamsdev

- **Streams Exchange**
  https://www.ibm.com/developerworks/mydeveloperworks/
  groups/service/html/communityview?communityUuid=d4e7dc
  8d-0efb-44ff-9a82-897202a3021e

Open-Source Toolkits

Open-source toolkits, operators, and so on can be found on multiple sites. The Streams exchange includes multiple URLs:

- **Streams operators**
  https://www.ibm.com/developerworks/mydeveloperworks/files/
  app?lang=en#/collection/09ddaa56-cd45-4e04-b880-d52a3ab630c0

- **Streams applications**
  https://www.ibm.com/developerworks/mydeveloperworks/files/
  app?lang=en#/collection/ef9f8aa9-240f-4854-aae3-ef3b065791da

There is also a third URL that includes tools. Refer to the main Streams Exchange page to find it, or you can find a reference to it in the InfoSphere Streams Playbook's Developer Corner page.

Also, a few locations on GitHub include open-source toolkits and examples:

- **IBMStreams**
  https://github.com/IBMStreams/

- **Streams toolkit for HBase**
  https://github.com/hildrum/StreamsToolkitForHBASE

- **Network content toolkit**
  https://github.com/ejpring/NetworkContentToolkit

- **Network packet toolkit**
  https://github.com/ejpring/NetworkPacketToolkit

- **Streams login script**
  https://github.com/christravis/streams-login-script

- **Synchronize toolkit**
  https://github.com/ejpring/SynchronizeToolkit

- **Linux shell toolkit**
  https://github.com/ejpring/LinuxShellToolkit

Sample Code

Sample code can be found in the InfoSphere Streams Quick Start Edition VMware image or on the Streams exchange at

> https://www.ibm.com/developerworks/mydeveloperworks/files/
> app?lang=en#/collection/ef9f8aa9-240f-4854-aae3-ef3b065791da

Streams-Related Articles

Sample code can be found in articles published on the IBM DeveloperWorks site at http://www.ibm.com/developerworks/library.

In the Zone drop-down box, select Information Management, and in the Keywords box, enter **Streams**. Once the results come back, you can sort them by date by clicking the Date header. This way, the list shows the most recent article first. These articles are of a technical nature, and several include sample code that supports the subject of the article.

Also, interesting high-level articles on Streams that are published regularly in the online IBM data magazine can be found at http://ibmdatamag.com/.

Internet of Things Articles

Chapter 2 mentioned several Internet of Things articles. Here are the references:

- **"Sonar Buoys Help Spot and Recognize Sharks Before It's Too Late"**
  http://gizmodo.com/sonar-buoys-help-spot-and-recognize-sharks-
  before-its-t-1598552194

- **"These Parking Meters Know If You're Driving a Gas-Guzzler"**
  http://www.businessweek.com/articles/2014-06-30/these-parking-
  meters-know-if-youre-driving-a-gas-guzzler

- **"Dueling Efforts to Let Connected Devices Talk Will Make It Tough for Them to Talk"**
  http://recode.net/2014/07/07/dueling-efforts-to-let-connected-
  devices-to-talk-will-make-it-tough-for-them-to-talk/

- **"These Printed Circuits Could Connect Any Object For Just a Few Cents"**
  http://gizmodo.com/these-printed-circuits-could-connect-any-object-
  for-jus-1598787729

- **"Is Your Android Device Telling the World Where You've Been?"** https://www.eff.org/deeplinks/2014/07/your-android-device-telling-world-where-youve-been

Smarter Planet

IBM has many initiatives around Smarter Planet. Chapter 2 mentioned some of these. Here is a link to the main page:

http://www.ibm.com/smarterplanet/us/en/topics/

Additional Skills Resources

InfoSphere BigInsights for Hadoop Community
Rely on the wide range of IBM experts, programs, and services that are available to help you take your Big Data skills to the next level. Participate with us online in the InfoSphere BigInsights for Hadoop Community. Find whitepapers; videos; demos; BigInsights downloads; links to Twitter, blogs, and Facebook pages; and more.

Visit **https://developer.ibm.com/hadoop/**

Big Data University
Big Data University.com makes Big Data education available to everyone, and starts a journey of discovery to change the world! Big Data technologies, such as Hadoop and Streams, paired with cloud computing, can enable even students to explore data that can lead to important discoveries in the health, environmental, and other industries.

Visit **http://bigdatauniversity.com**

IBM Certification and Mastery Exams
Find industry-leading professional certification and mastery exams. New mastery exams are now available for InfoSphere BigInsights and InfoSphere Streams.

Visit **www-03.ibm.com/certify/mastery_tests**

Twitter
For the latest news and information as it happens, follow us on Twitter: **@IBMBigData**, **@Hadoop_Dev**, and **@IBMAnalytics**

developerWorks
On developerWorks, you'll find deep technical articles and tutorials that can help you build your skills to the mastery level. Also find downloads to free and trial versions of software to try today.

Visit **www.ibm.com/developerworks/analytics/**

Blogs

A team of experts regularly write blogs related to the full spectrum of Big Data topics. Bookmark the "Stream Computing" page and check often to stay on top of industry trends.

Visit **www.ibmbigdatahub.com/technology/stream-computing** or **www.ibmbigdatahub.com/technology/all**

This is part of The Big Data & Analytics Hub (ibmbigdatahub.com) that is populated with the content from thought leaders, subject matter experts, and Big Data practitioners (both IBM and third-party thinkers). The Big Data & Analytics Hub is your source for information, content, and conversation regarding Big Data analytics for the enterprise.

IBM Data Magazine

IBM Data magazine delivers substantive, high-quality content on the latest data management developments and IBM advances, as well as creates a strong community of the world's top information management professionals. It vividly demonstrates how the smart use of data and information advances broad business success, providing the context that enables data management professionals at all levels to make more informed choices and create innovative, synchronized, agile solutions. The magazine's clear, in-depth technical advice and hands-on examples show readers how to immediately improve productivity and performance. At the same time, expert commentary clearly articulates how advanced technical capabilities benefit the people and processes throughout an organization.

Visit **http://ibmdatamag.com**

IBM Redbooks

IBM Redbooks publications are developed and published by the IBM International Technical Support Organization (ITSO). The ITSO develops and delivers skills, technical know-how, and materials to IBM technical professionals, business partners, clients, and the marketplace in general.

Visit **http://ibm.com/redbooks**